The Ralph Story

My Search for The Lady of Shalott

Martyn Bradley

WELLINGTON

BOOKS

The Lady of Shalott, 1888. John William Waterhouse. Tate. Photo: Tate.

For my daughter, Abi, without whose encouragement the quest would never have been completed.

This story is not an autobiography. There is not much to be found here that does not relate directly to the central quest. Whilst I have included some social history and endeavoured to highlight some of the relevant attitudes and laws which have changed over time, there is very little to do with either my working life or my music, both of which have occupied many, many hours but have had little influence on the years of searching.

All related within the story is true as far as I can remember. The birth story as it was originally told to me by my mum in 1962 is 'word for word'.

Any errors are purely down to a lapse of memory over the intervening years. I have changed some names to protect the identities of individuals who may still be with us.

Chapter 1
The gold watch

I think I should begin my story as Martyn Bradley at twelve years old, for that is when the bombshell dropped.

I enjoyed the things you would expect any twelve-year-old boy in England in the early 1960s to enjoy. Eagle and Lion comics dropped through the letterbox every week. I collected postage stamps. I played the side-drum in the Boys' Brigade band, and most of all I enjoyed playing outside with my large group of local friends.

Sidcup in Kent in those days retained a small-town feel and housed reminders that the war was not long over. The first money I ever 'earned' was in helping to demolish a nearby air-raid shelter in the crescent just off the main road. I must have been nine or ten and all the gang were involved. Although I remember it as great fun, it was probably extremely dangerous!

My immediate family was not large – Mum and Dad, and me. I had three cousins whom I liked but who lived way up north and for most of the time didn't exist in my world. On the rare occasions they visited, we had big family gatherings at grandparents' houses where we children had to be on our best behaviour – or else!

At that age I wasn't much interested in my aunts and uncles and there seemed to be a lot of them. Dad's father had married one of four sisters who all lived around the Sidcup area, which is why my parents had settled there after I came along. Life was great and I was an extremely happy child. I had passed the 11+ exam and went to a very good school.

One of the most important things for me at that time, and something that has remained of equal importance throughout my life, was a sense of belonging. I was never happier than when I was part of a group, and joined just about every available club: sports teams, Sunday School, the Boys' Brigade, the Saturday morning pictures (ABC Minors) crowd. I worked hard, played hard, and enjoyed a wonderful childhood.

It was when I was twelve I first encountered the word 'adopted'. In September 1961, I was a new boy at Cray Valley Technical School. In our year was a boy, Colin, whose parents had been killed in a road accident when he was younger. We became good friends. He lived with his grandparents, and he often talked about how strict they were, not letting him take part in things the rest of us took for granted. The incident I remember best was the school production of Gilbert and Sullivan's *Trial by Jury*. We first and second years all went along to the auditions, got parts and were thrilled that we were to be part of a prestigious event in the school calendar. Colin had to withdraw from the production after the first rehearsal because it meant he got home late from school and this had upset some routine his grandparents lived to. I remember him being so angry and saying his real parents would have enjoyed his being in the production, but of course his grandparents 'had only adopted him'. I realised his grandparents were now bringing him up but it was as if 'adopted' meant something rather nasty, especially in a twelve-year-old's mind.

The bombshell dropped a little later that same year. The

extended family had gathered to celebrate Christmas and the birthday of my father's grandfather. A very rich, strict and supposedly religious man, he gave all his great-grandchildren an inscribed gold watch for Christmas. All except me.

The reason given to my parents was that I was 'adopted'. I vaguely remember the rows this caused. In fact, my parents never spoke to him again. From then on, there was always an atmosphere when we were with any of his daughters, who we referred to as my great aunts, and the bad feeling must have had an effect on me in that I remember those times so well even now.

Mum and Dad were very involved in the Baptist church. Mum sang in the choir and had run the Girl Guides until a few years previous, and Dad was the Sunday School superintendent so they weren't exactly the sort of people to bear grudges for little or no reason. It must have been a really bad time for them and I didn't understand the 'adopted' thing that had caused so much ill-feeling and resentment. OK, I hadn't got my watch, but there was obviously some matter of fairness or principle at work somewhere.

I can't remember exactly how long after this event it was that I asked what 'adopted' really meant – perhaps just a week or so – but I can vividly remember finding out!

It was Mum who told me. I probably asked her rather than Dad because she always seemed to explain things so clearly. We were very close and discussed most things quite openly and in some depth. At that time world affairs such as Yuri Gagarin's flight into space and the increasing tension in Cuba were the sort of things that got us going, but until that day I had never once mentioned gold watches or adoption. She must have had a lot of confidence in my ability to deal with the story as she certainly didn't hold back on the details. I can remember waiting with some trepidation in the lounge while she went upstairs to fetch some papers she thought I should see.

She first explained what adoption meant – that I was someone else's child but that I was now part of the Bradley family and they were bringing me up. I was legally their child although Mum hadn't actually given birth to me. I then heard a story that I was to hear many times over the years. It all rang true and it never changed.

I wasn't Martyn Bradley at all: I was born Ralph Allan Wellington on October 8th 1949 at The Haven, a Home for unmarried mothers and babies run by the Baptist Missionary Society in Yateley, just outside of London and near Aldershot. My real mother was Dorothy Ruth Wellington. The Home had told my parents that she was the 16-year-old daughter of a missionary family in Leopoldville, capital of the Belgian Congo in Africa. Trouble had erupted in that country and Dorothy Ruth had been one of the victims of an unprecedented attack on a white mission station. Being young and evidently very pretty, she had formed a prime target. My father could have been any one of a number of individuals. There had also been some deaths but it was not known whether any of the Wellington family were victims. Dorothy Ruth had been shipped back from Africa to England on her own with arrangements made for her to give birth at The Haven in order to avoid further scandal to the family and the Missionary Society, and for her own safety.

Mum knew all the details, as told her by The Haven: Dorothy had come by ship into Southampton and had been taken to The Haven by another missionary, a friend of the Wellingtons, who was home on furlough. We had provided accommodation at home for missionaries on furlough and so I knew this meant they were back in England having a rest from their overseas work. Mum fetched the original adoption information which showed my real mother's name and The Haven's record of my birth and development during my first weeks of life, so I knew it was all true. Mum explained that she couldn't have any children of her own. She had conceived some years earlier but had miscarried very late in the pregnancy. Complications had left adoption as the only option for having and raising a child. They loved me as if I were their own, and Mum hoped above all else that, having been told the incredible truth, it would not change the love I had for her and Dad.

I reassured her that of course it didn't change a thing. But I cried. I cried a lot, in fact – not for myself or for Mum or our family in Sidcup, but for Dorothy Ruth. What had she endured so far from England and how on earth did she manage to cope with all that happened to her following such an outrage? Mum loved the Pre-Raphaelites and we had a large print of *The Lady of Shalott* by John William Waterhouse on the wall in the lounge – the beautiful young maiden sailing away in the boat not knowing what lies before her.

'The Lady of Shalott', 1888. John William Waterhouse. Tate. Photo: Tate.

Following my 'finding out', it always represented Dorothy Ruth, my mother, escaping over the water to an unknown life, frightened and alone. I still get quite emotional when I see that painting. Of course, it now crops up absolutely everywhere!

I had so many questions to ask Mum that day. I wanted to know all about The Haven, I wanted to know why I had been chosen for the Bradley family instead of all the other babies at the home, but the first question – and by far the most important to me – was 'What was my real mother like?' Mum could not answer. She was, I remember, very emotional at this point and explained that it was a strict policy of The Haven, and indeed all homes from which babies were adopted in those days, that birth mothers and adoptive parents were not allowed any interaction and therefore did not meet. All the information Mum had shared had been obtained from The Haven itself, and apart from the two pieces of paper which listed my birth date, my real mother's name, my weights on various days and the date of my legal adoption, there was nothing else. Thank goodness Mum had the mind to keep those sheets of paper safe. She gave them to me on that day, and they became the most valuable of my possessions.

I think Mum had known the day would come when she would have to go through this and, now it was over, she seemed to radiate a new level of happiness. I remember being left in the front room on my own for some time after I heard this amazing story, reflecting on its content. It was a tearful time.

So then, finally, I knew why I hadn't got my watch! It was to do with real family relations, fathers and sons and the sharing of a common blood, things I was not part of in the mind of my great-grandfather. I did not belong.

I wiped away the tears, looked at the Lady of Shalott and vowed to myself that I would find my real mother.

However long it took.

THE BAPTIST UNION OF GREAT BRITAIN AND IRELAND
(BAPTIST WOMEN'S LEAGUE)

GENERAL SECRETARY:
THE REV. M. E. AUBREY, C.H., M.A.

ORGANISING & DEPUTATION SECRETARY
MISS E. L. CHAPPLE

THE HAVEN
(HOME FOR MOTHERS AND BABIES)

MATRON:
MISS A. K. FINNEY,
S.R.N., S.C.M., M.T.D., D.N. (LOND.)

TEL. YATELEY 3107

VIGO LANE,
YATELEY,
NR. CAMBERLEY

R A L P H.

Date of Birth 8.10.1949.   Birth Weight. 8 lb.7½ ozs.

At 25.11.49. 10 lbs.10.ozs.

Feeds: 5 level measures Half-Cream "Cow & Gate"

5½ ozs. or 11 Tablespoons. hot boiled water.

(Four-hourly, the last feed 9.30 p.m.)

Orange Juice - ½ Teaspoon to 1 oz. water.
(Given by spoon from small cup......4.45 p.m.

Cod Liver Oil - ½ Teaspoonful by spoon before 10 a.m.
and 6 p.m. feeds.

Baby has been successfully vaccinated and circumcised. Sits on

chamber after every feed. Will soon require Full-Cream Cow & Gate.

Martyn Bradley

A.C.A. 4.—*Adoption Order in respect of an infant.*
(Rule 18 of the Adoption of Children (County Court) Rules, 1949.)

In the   BROMLEY   **County Court.**

No. F 245

IN THE MATTER OF THE ADOPTION OF CHILDREN ACTS, 1926 TO 1949,

AND

(SEAL)

(1) Enter name(s) and surname as shown in the heading of Form A.C.A. 1.

IN THE MATTER OF (¹) _RALPH ALLAN WELLINGTON_ AN INFANT.

Application having been made by _GERALD LESLIE RICHARD BRADLEY_

by occupation _RAILWAY CLERK_ resident

at _19 NORTHCOTE ROAD, SIDCUP, KENT,_ and

domiciled in England/Wales [and _DOROTHY MARY BRADLEY_ his wife]

(hereinafter called the ~~applicant~~/applicants) for an order under the Adoption of Children Acts, 1926

to 1949, authorising ~~him/her/~~them to adopt _RALPH ALLAN WELLINGTON_, an

infant, the ~~child/~~adopted child of _DOROTHY RUTH WELLINGTON_ /

_____ and _____ ;

And the said _RALPH ALLAN WELLINGTON_ (hereinafter called the infant)

being of the _MALE_ sex, and never having been married ;

And the ~~applicant/one of the~~ applicants

having attained the age of twenty-five years and being at least twenty-one years older than the infant *or*

having attained the age of twenty-one years and being a relative of the infant within the meaning of the said Acts *or*

~~being the mother/father of the infant ;~~

(2) Delete where there is no change of name.

(3) Delete this entry—
(a) if the infant is not identified with a person whose birth is registered in the Registers of Births in England, Wales or Scotland, or in a Register of Births abroad kept by the Registrar General ;
(b) if the infant has previously been adopted. Where the infant is identified with a person whose birth is registered in any such register other than the Registers of Births in England or Wales, modify the entry accordingly.

[And the names by which the infant is to be known being _MARTYN RICHARD_

BRADLEY] (²)

[And it having been proved to the satisfaction of the judge that the infant is identical with

RALPH ALAN, to whom the entry numbered _393_

and made on the _19th October_ 19 _49_, in the Register

of Births for the registration district of _ALDERSHOT_

and sub-district of _HARTLEY WINTNEY_ in the county of

SOUTHAMPTON relates] (³) ;

8

And the [probable](⁴) date of the birth of the infant appearing to be the

(4) Delete
" probable ",
where the
precise date of
the infant's birth
is proved.
8th October _____ 19 49.

[And the infant having been previously the subject of an adoption order dated the

(5) Delete
except where the
infant has
previously been
adopted.
_____ 19____, of which particulars are entered in

the Adopted Children Register](⁵) ;

And all the consents required by the said Acts being obtained or dispensed with ;

It is ordered that the applicant/applicants be authorised to adopt the infant ;

[And the following payment or reward is sanctioned :

_____]

[And as regards costs it is ordered that :

_____]

And it is directed that the Registrar General shall make in the Adopted Children Register an
entry recording the adoption in accordance with the particulars set out in the Schedule to this order.

[And it is further directed that the Registrar General shall cause the said entry in the Register
of Births to be marked with the word " adopted "](³).

[And it is further directed that the Registrar General shall cause the previous entry in the Adopted
Children Register relating to the infant to be marked with the word " re-adopted "](⁶).

Dated the ___18th___ day of _____April_____ 19 50.

Registrar.

(6) Where a
probable date of
birth is specified
in the body of
the order, enter
that date without
qualification.
If the infant is
one of twins,
include, if
possible, the
hour as well as
the date of birth.

(7) Where there
is a change,
enter only the
names by which
the infant is to
be known.

HOURS OF ATTENDANCE {
at the Court Office }
from 10 a.m. till 2.30 p.m., except on
when the Office will be open from

SCHEDULE TO FORM No. 4

Date(6) and country of birth of child	Name and surname of child(7)	Sex of child	Name and surname, address and occupation of adopter or adopters	Date of adoption order and description of court by which made
8th Oct. 1949 England	~~MARTYN~~ Richard Bradley	male	GERALD LESLIE RICHARD BRADLEY 19 NORTHCOTE ROAD, SIDCUP, KENT RAILWAY CLERK AND DOROTHY MARY BRADLEY HOUSEWIFE	18th April, 1950 BROMLEY COUNTY COURT.

(P2207) Wt.38181 1339 1.50 Hw.

Chapter 2
A bit of background

To understand fully the boy I was at twelve, we must now return to, and start from, the beginning.

The first thing I have realised in putting together the story of my earliest years is that it covers a period from which I have no memories. I have no personal knowledge of either of the first two houses in which we lived as a family. After my collection from The Haven in November 1949, my first residence was at 19 Northcote Road, Sidcup, Kent. My adoptive parents' extended families had all lived in the area since the later part of the 19th century and consequently they had set up house there immediately after the war. They were married with a wartime wedding in 1940, and it was during the next few years that they discovered they could not have children of their own. This was evidently due to a childhood illness in my mother – I believe it was a rare form of scarlet fever but I'm not sure if I've remembered that correctly. Anyway, I arrived in Sidcup towards the end of 1949 but the family moved to Dovercourt near Harwich on the Essex coast almost immediately. This was due to the job opportunities with all the ports reopening after the war. I was never sure what Dad actually did for a living, but it was something to do with the railways and communications. He worked at the big seaport at Parkeston Quay.

My earliest memories are of Dovercourt. We rented and lived in Old Vicarage Farm. I have the vaguest of memories here: friends, the Chilvers, arriving after the great sea surge and coastal floods of January 1953. Their house was flooded when the seawall gave way and they lived with us for a while.

We stayed in Old Vicarage Farm for two years and then my parents bought our first home in King George's Avenue. I think this was about the time I started school and would have been in 1954. I can remember lots from this period onward. I recall the concrete blocks for war defence being removed from the beaches and put in piles by the side of the local football pitch, which I walked past every day en route to school. It was exciting stuff and a great place for young boys to play, though I once fell off and still have a nasty scar on my right knee! I also remember piles of mines which had been retrieved from the North Sea.

I first went to school at Second Avenue Primary School and I hated it. I guess I was five years old and loved the sea by then. School just got in the way. Mum used to meet me from school and I remember going straight to the beach from there, swimming and playing on the sand. I remember it as happening all the time, but I'm sure it didn't! My first love was at this school. Her name was Michelle Wright. She was beautiful and always had her hair in pigtails. I was madly in love with her. We were going to stow away in a ship together from Harwich – we had it all planned out. Isn't life simple when you're five!

Being in Dovercourt made us very popular with my various aunts and uncles who lived in towns inland and far from seaside holiday spots. We always seemed to have family members visiting us for day trips or full weekends if they brought their children with them and came as a family. The many cousins visited more than once or twice and most of the family photographs of this period of the early 1950s show us cousins playing happily on the beaches or in the sea. These early formative years were blissful and went by without a care in the world. I really was blessed with a wonderful family and an idyllic early childhood.

We lived in Dovercourt until I was six or just seven. It was a great place to grow up, and I remember being very upset when we moved away to Crawley. I knew by now that Dad was a radar specialist. A new job had come up. Crawley was one of the 'New Towns', and only half built when we arrived. I don't have vivid memories of this place in the same way as I do of Dovercourt and I think we were there for just two years. Most of the time was spent playing on the building sites and 'Tizer-bottling'. All the fizzy-drink bottles in those days were returnable to the shop and you got threepence back on the bottle. My great memory of Crawley is going round all the sites getting the Tizer and lemonade bottles from the workmen and taking them back to the shops for them. We collected threepence for every bottle and were never short of money for chocolate and ice creams. Apart from that, Crawley is instantly forgettable. Everyone was new in the New Town and there being no other close family in the neighbourhood, and few organisations for young people, I never really felt part of anything.

After two years, Dad got another job and we moved back to Sidcup where most of the extended family members still lived. We lived at 68 Longlands Road and I started at yet another school – Longlands Primary. I loved it here and it was a super place for a nine-year-old boy. I had loads of friends who all lived close by and we were into everything. It was here in Sidcup again that I really developed a joy in the sense of belonging. I loved music and got my first guitar for a birthday present, although I didn't take to it then and didn't play properly until I was about sixteen. Saturday mornings were always spent at the cinema for 'Saturday Morning Pictures Club'. This was common all over the UK: a mixture of children's feature films, cartoons and the next instalment of whichever serial was on. I can remember titles such as *The Purple Monster* and, my favourite, *The Phantom Empire* starring Gene Autry. A whole crowd of us from Longlands School used to go together. I seem to remember that it cost sixpence. I became a cinema 'Monitor' after a while, which meant I had a job – selling ice-cream or selling the ABC badges to the queue. For this I got in free! One of my jobs was to change the posters in the big display boards outside the front of the cinema, which showed what was on each week. I must have done this for over a year when I asked if I could keep one of the old ones – which I did – but oh how I wish I'd kept them all. *Ben Hur*, *North by Northwest* and *West Side Story* were three in my collection of probably over a hundred pristine originals. If only I knew where they were now.

My greatest passion during this period leading up to being twelve was being a member of the Boys' Brigade and drummer in the Brigade band. One of my aunties had bought me a tin drum for my 4th birthday and I had always wanted to play the drum properly. We had band practice every Thursday night at the church hall in Woodside Road and I loved it. Church Parades were the first Sunday in every month and I was never prouder as a kid than when we were marching up Sidcup Main Road with the full band playing. I had a brief membership in the Scouts during this period but,

without a band, it was not the same. Sadly, I have no pictures of this time at all except the dreaded annual school portraits.

I can remember asking and being allowed to take my drum home – I was very keen. It was set up on a stand in my bedroom and the first thing I did when I got home from school each day was to run through what I'd learnt at Boys' Brigade the week before – time and time again. Mum was usually very supportive of all my ventures but on this occasion I think it only lasted a few weeks before it was banned and, sadly, the drum returned to the Boys' Brigade cupboard in the church hall.

So there you have it, everything about life was just wonderful and, although finding out my true history was a monumental bombshell, it didn't really affect my immediate family. I loved them dearly, but I was now on a mission to discover my birth mother and family.

Chapter 3
My search begins

To say that everything changed after the revelations of Christmas 1961 and January 1962 would not be entirely true, although I always felt a little different from that time onward.

I had resolved to find my mother and my real family but had absolutely no idea how to go about it. One thing I had definitely decided was to keep the quest to myself. I never told my adoptive parents that I was even interested in finding Dorothy Ruth.

Looking back now, some of my earliest attempts to seek out information were extremely naïve and almost laughable, but to a young teenager appeared probably quite realistic. I looked up 'Wellington' in every telephone directory I came across, especially in other areas of the country we visited as a family. I soon found this to be one of my not so brilliant ideas, but probably thought I really was achieving something, until it was pointed out to me by one of the 'clever' boys at school that the reference section of the local library had lots of directories, and certainly those for the whole London area. I abandoned this line of enquiry on discovering just how many Wellingtons there were. I didn't even know, of course, whether they had returned from the Congo. So I decided that people were most likely the best source of information, especially those with common interests with the Wellington family – the missionaries.

During the early part of the 1960s, my family were very much involved with both the Church and the Baptist Missionary Society, and this continued until we moved away from Sidcup in 1964. We often heard stories from the missions in Africa during the church services on Sundays, as missionaries home on furlough were invited to the church as guest speakers. I can remember speaking to these visitors on more than one occasion, hoping to hear any recent news from the Belgian Congo and thus being able to ask further questions, but none of those I spoke to were from that particular country. I had developed quite an interest myself, especially after hearing my own story, and when asked to do an extended piece of work at school on 'A Hero from Recent History', I chose David Livingstone, although at the time I was probably more fascinated by his explorations into the interior of the mysterious continent than his missionary work. I wrote about the meeting of previously undiscovered tribes, of shooting the rapids on the Zambezi River, and I remember drawing a picture of his discovery of the Victoria Falls.

It wasn't only Africa that featured. Mum had met Gladys Aylward on several occasions and had also heard her give talks on her work in the Far East. Consequently, I also produced a big project at school on 'The Small Woman', telling the tale of her mission in China and her leading the children to safety over the Shanxi mountains from Yangcheng to Xian. I was riveted by Gladys's story and, although I never met her personally, I felt great admiration for her, so small in stature but able to achieve so much through such a deep belief that what she was doing was right. I thought maybe most missionaries were the same; it was a calling: my real mother's family would have the same qualities! A year or so later Mum, Dad and I watched when Gladys appeared on television as the subject of *This Is Your Life* with Eamonn Andrews. The researchers had tracked down several of the children she had led to safety during the Japanese invasion of 1938. They had not seen each other for over 25 years, and it is still one of the greatest and most emotional pieces of television I have ever seen. It should be remembered that it was a time in England when heroes of the empire and achievement in general were very much a part of the educational curriculum, especially in the primary schools.

But I now had my own hero to research, and had embarked on the biggest project of my life.

Dad had the *Telegraph* delivered every day and I always scanned it for news concerning the Belgian Congo. Any that did appear was not necessarily good news, and mainly covered riots over the country's new independence or other trouble involving United Nations troops who had been sent in. I wondered, in the light of so much violence, whether the Wellington family were still there? I wrote my first letter requesting information during late 1963 or early 1964. I am vague about specific times during this early research – the memories have faded somewhat – but of this episode I am certain: it was my third year at Cray Valley school and I recruited Colin's help by use of his address. By then he knew that I, like him, was adopted, and although I had not divulged any details of my real mother, he was keen to help. I wrote to the Baptist Missionary Society in London requesting any information they could supply about the Wellington missionary family who had been in Leopoldville during the 1940s, especially their present whereabouts.

The first reply was quick. It arrived via Colin at school registration and I can remember him joking about 'the letter that will change your life'. It was, however, simply a short note thanking me for my enquiry and stating that it had been passed to the relevant department to be dealt with in due course. I felt good:

my request had been received and the wheels were rolling. I had visions of opening the next letter to find my quest completed in one of life's eureka moments.

It was a very long interval between replies from the Missionary Society, and I can remember having my emotions torn in differing directions: feeling increasingly dismayed by the lack of information, but also thinking that the passing of time might be due to them having to collect the relevant facts for me. Colin was the only person who knew anything whatsoever about my search, and consequently he was the one I could talk to. I always thought he was very astute and had a way of empathising that was not common amongst teenage schoolboys. He seemed to understand what I was going through and, when the second reply arrived, he kept hold of it and didn't pass it to me until the morning break: a much longer period of time than the five-minute registration. He knew I would need time to take in the contents, whether good or bad. I was angry at first – I had waited a long time for any news and I wanted it immediately – but once I had opened the letter, Colin must have read the increasing disappointment shown in my face and quietly moved off to talk to other friends.

The reply, which was typed rather than handwritten, was lengthy and contained an in-depth explanation of why the organisation could not give out specific information on families who were, or had been, involved in work for the mission. Members of specific families who wished to contact missionary relatives should address correspondence to the specific missionary concerned, care of the Baptist Missionary Society, who would forward the items. They concluded by thanking me for my letter and suggesting that I allow my parents to make any future contact. I should have guessed, really, by looking at the envelope: it was addressed to Master M. Bradley! At the time I was devastated, not so much by the fact that I had no further information but because I had lost faith in my ability to communicate on an adult level. I was so angry. How dare they treat me like a child! But, of course, that's exactly what I was.

I can't remember how long I brooded over the contents of that letter, but it was certainly one of the bleakest emotional periods of my life. I'm sure the more one thinks about a situation the more complex it tends to become, and at that time I began to doubt whether I could achieve any satisfactory outcome in looking for Dorothy Ruth. Visions of some great reunion with my real mother began to give way to thoughts of rejection. Was it an episode in her life she would hate to be reminded of? After all, it was thirteen years previous and she would now be twenty-nine! Would I be a disappointment if she did meet me? The main problem was that I was keeping it all to myself and bottling it up inside. I needed to talk to someone.

The leaders of our Boys' Brigade at church were some of the few adults I really felt comfortable talking to, so I decided to approach our musical director after band practice, which was held every Thursday night in the Christchurch hall. Arthur, the musical director and band leader, was a special friend, and it was in him I confided.

A huge Scot with a big moustache and an even larger beard, Arthur was an unforgettable character. I remember him as quite old but he was probably in his forties. As far as the Boys' Brigade was concerned, he was a strict disciplinarian and didn't suffer fools gladly, but he also understood young people and was a great listener. I did know he was also a solicitor – although, at the time of asking him to hear me out, I didn't know that would help at all. We went to his house which was just around the corner from the church hall, and over a cup of tea I poured out the whole story. I think I left out some of the lurid details of Dorothy Ruth's experiences and her young age but, apart from those facts, he heard the lot. I can still hear his 'Whoa!' in a broad Scots accent, followed by: 'I suppose you're asking me what you ought to do next, laddie?' Where the conversation went beyond that I have no recollection, but I do remember that we met again after another band practice a couple of weeks later. Being a solicitor, he probably wanted time to get all his facts correct: 'I'll need a bit of time to think about this one, Martyn!'

I looked up to Arthur and valued his opinions greatly, but when we met on that second occasion his view of the situation was difficult to take on board, especially for an emotionally involved teenager. Arthur wasn't one to 'beat about the bush', although I remember his compassion. His immediate advice was to drop it – at least until I was an adult – and then to assess what I really wanted. He pointed out that as an adopted child I had no legal right to any information concerning my real mother or her immediate family and any attempt to trace them was going to be frowned upon from all involved. I would get little help, if any. (This was not to change until the Children Act of 1975.) I had been given up for adoption by my real mother, whose family had instigated the whole procedure. As far as Arthur knew, there was rarely any contact in adoption cases between adoptive parents and birth mothers. This, evidently, wasn't actual law but was the usual situation designed to protect both families.

Arthur also pointed out that he knew me as Martyn Bradley, a member of a family he knew well and respected as active members of the church. I had always been, or had appeared to be, a very happy and contented child with a solid set of values which were based on the upbringing which Mum and Dad had provided – a happy family, in fact. He could see how passionate I was with my quest, but didn't recommend embarking on a journey which could possibly end in changing all that. One of his favourite sayings was: 'Count your blessings, laddie!' I thought maybe I should, and then the emotion took hold, and his drummer burst into tears!

Recovering from that meeting with Arthur was not easy. One

of the choruses we used to sing at Boys' Brigade, especially on camps, was: 'Count your blessings, name them one by one'. As I reflected on Arthur's advice, I did just that. My early life had indeed produced many blessings. I was a very happy boy, blessed with many talents and abilities. I should be content and grateful. I'm sure I was, but I just could not remove the passionate desire to discover my real roots. Was I being very stupid, should I be thoroughly content? Life was emotional turmoil.

It was at this time that I began to realise that the Bradleys had not become my adoptive parents purely by chance. I didn't know how the adoption process worked but they had surely been through some sort of selection procedure, matching up their values with those sought by The Haven together with the Wellington family. Even if the families never met, there must have been some selection and vetting of prospective adoptees. I really didn't know but came to the conclusion that my very special parents had been well selected and were definitely blessing number one.

Arthur must have had quite an effect on my overall mindset, and I relaxed at that time into a relatively stable period in my development. Until, that is, another bombshell was dropped in my way with the announcement that we were to move house. This was not simply a move just up the road, but to a totally different town. My parents viewed this as simply another change and improvement in our life, but for me this was devastating. Dad, who was a technical author at the time, was forming his own business with two other partners, and once this had been finalised, we would be moving to the company's location: Dartford in Kent.

My only memory of this house move is of the actual day of the move itself. It must have been just before we travelled, because the rooms were empty and the house was silent. Why I had ended up looking around the empty house I do not know, but the thing I can remember vividly is the empty space on the wall where *The Lady of Shalott* had hung. The space it once occupied was much darker than the wallpaper around it, which had faded over the years. What hadn't faded was my resolve to discover my mother and her family.

Chapter 4
Dartford – bands and blues

My time in Dartford coincided with that period in life which can at best be described as 'formative' but that adults would far more accurately call 'awkward!' Between ages thirteen and eighteen, I was no different to the rest of the teenage rebellion of the 1960s.

Drumming in the Boys' Brigade had sparked one of the great joys of my life and I decided I really wanted to play drums in other spheres – i.e., a band. I loved jazz at that time and, when I was thirteen or fourteen, Dad bought me a small drum-kit and sorted out lessons for me, with a man who turned out to be one of the best jazz drummers in London. I'm not sure how the contact was there originally – perhaps a friend of a friend – but I had a series of lessons with an irritable, almost miserable, person called Phil Seamen. I can remember him as an absolute pain but he was a wonderful player. The lessons weren't regular. He used to show me something and then say: 'When you can do that without thinking about it, come back.' My memories aren't clear but I know on more than one occasion he wasn't happy and told me to go away until I'd done it properly. Apart from doing numerous West-End shows, Phil Seamen appeared regularly at the London jazz clubs. I used to get the train to London to see him play with his quartet at the Royal Oak in Tooley Street; just wonderful music.

I joined my first group in 1965 when I was sixteen. It was called 'The Blues Element'. We did the usual round of local gigs at church youth clubs and village-hall dances. The band became quite well-known in the North Kent area and the dances were always packed – it was great fun and a time I remember vividly. The band's families were amazing throughout this time. We were all too young to have any transport of our own so our dads used to take it in turns to drive us to gigs and back. It wasn't until much later that I realised just how supportive they had been; often driving long distances to collect us and all the gear – amazing!

Some days you never forget. Chris, one of the guitarists in the band and in my class at school, was a very close friend and at the time became my 'Quest Confidante'. Chris was also adopted and had discovered this when he was twelve or thirteen but, unlike me, had no desire to discover his origins. He was surprised that I even knew the name of my real mother and where I had been born and assured me that this was quite unusual, normally being shrouded in secrecy. He had broached the subject on one occasion with his parents – I think when they told him of his adoption – and believed no information was available except that his real mother was no longer alive and had been gravely ill prior to his birth. He advised, very strongly, to leave things as they were and not to delve, although I remember him being extremely interested in my story.

Chris's dad was much older than mine and I always thought him to be the epitome of the 'wise old man'. On one glorious summer Saturday in 1965, our normal band practice didn't happen for some reason so Chris instead invited me to tea at his family's beautiful cottage in the country: the perfect location for what was to follow.

Chris's dad was as jovial as ever throughout tea and afterwards offered to show me around the garden, casually suggesting Chris might like to help his mum with the washing-up. Once on our own, his whole attitude changed. Chris had obviously talked about our discussions and had started to ask questions. Evidently this was strictly taboo in their family and I received a lecture on responsibility and a warning not to encourage Chris to research his birth family. He also suggested that any research on my part into the whereabouts of my birth mother's family was both ill-conceived and possibly dangerous. My mother had given me up for a reason. The decision must have been heart-wrenching and she had now had sixteen years to get over it – or, at least, to come to terms with it. My intervention could only cause distress and anguish to her and those in her current life. Chris's dad sent a clear message: if you are sensible, leave it alone. As far as their family was concerned, his real mother was dead and that was that. For the first time in my life, I looked into a respected adult's eyes and knew he was lying. Our tour of the garden ended by Chris's father suggesting it wouldn't be a good idea to tell Chris of our 'conversation'. On returning to the cottage, things carried on as if the incident had never happened: Chris's father was a brilliant actor. I never did mention it to Chris and we parted company in 1967 on finishing school. I never saw him again.

The incident with Chris's father left me angry but I wondered deep down if he was correct in his thinking. Although he had been seething, his message and eloquent delivery had the desired effect. For the first time, I seriously wondered if I should continue with my quest. Indeed, my mother would be much older and a very different person to the one who gave birth to the unwanted son.

Or was I unwanted? Had events and her family contrived to force the adoption? Had she really wanted to keep me? Would she have kept me, had the situation been different? Was she now happily married with a husband and children? If she had more children, how would my discovery affect them?

So many questions. I entered a prolonged mental turmoil and didn't recover quickly. I brooded over the entire situation for a long time, possibly years, because it was not until I left for college in 1968 that I rekindled my desire to find the truth.

Fellowship of Youth, 1967

Apart from attending school and playing in the blues band, I filled the years in Dartford by satisfying that instinctive sense of belonging and it was during that time that I made life-long friends. The Baptist church was miles away but the local Presbyterian church was within easy walking distance, and had a youth club, so it was to there I gravitated in the mid 1960s. The F.O.Y. (Fellowship of Youth) became an extended family at this time as we did so much together: Church and F.O.Y. meetings on Sundays, Youth Club on Thursdays and various get-togethers at other times. We engaged in the activities you would expect of healthy teenagers: playing and listening to music, dancing, parties and generally annoying our parents. Discussions were lively and covered a multitude of subject matters: we talked about God, growing up, politics, music and who was going out with whom. It was a wonderful group of friends, but in all that time I never divulged my quest except to my best buddy, Dave Chandler. His was a friendship that would mature with the years and last until the present day.

Chapter 5
College in Chichester, West Sussex

In the Autumn of 1968, I exchanged family life in industrial Dartford for the freedom and challenges of a residential college in the leafy comfort of Chichester. I had drifted somewhat during the previous few years and, after gaining a surprisingly good set of qualifications at school, had spent a rather wasteful year at art college. It was a time when I really did need to make some serious decisions concerning what I wanted to do with my life and where I should go next. The most positive aspect of that period is that I further developed my interest in music and became immersed in it. I played the guitar reasonably well and drumming had continued to be one of my major interests. After a lot of soul-searching and discussion with friends and family, I decided I would utilize my creative skills and become a teacher.

I arrived at Chichester's Bishop Otter College with my guitar and a battered suitcase containing the necessities of life together with the most important things of the time: my clothes, the prescribed coursebooks, my favourite LP records and the two sheets of adoption information given to me by my mother all those years ago. Also, there were addresses to which I had written years earlier only to receive either no reply at all, or – as was more common – a negative reply of some sort. This secret stash contained among the replies the fateful letter which Colin had received on my behalf in 1963, which had been hidden away in the bowels of my bedroom in Dartford. Having left home, I now had the freedom to investigate and research as I wished. Trouble was, I had absolutely no idea how to proceed and the pace of life in Chichester meant I did no research at all during the first two years. There were many talented musicians at the college and once I had managed to transport my drums down to Sussex, I joined a jazz quartet.

It was always the case that you could tell an awful lot about a particular student simply by looking at the interior of their room. Mine was no exception and would have mirrored my personality: firstly, it was extremely untidy! The diverse contents were a direct reflection on lifestyle and mine was soon filled with the paraphernalia associated with art and music. Various instruments littered the room and the walls were covered by posters advertising jazz and rock concerts. One picture, however, stood out. Chichester, like most cities, had its share of second-hand and junk shops and it was on one Saturday browsing excursion that I found, in amongst a stock of old dusty framed pictures, a print of *The Lady of Shalott*. Once I cleaned the grime from the glass, it adorned my bedroom wall for my entire college life. More than once, the picture was commented on by friends as being slightly incongruous alongside images of The Rolling Stones and Dizzy Gillespie.

Bishop Otter was a Church of England funded college named after one of the great Bishops of Chichester (he's buried in the Cathedral) and was a very rich institution in those days with wonderful buildings and gardens and a huge art collection. The facilities, art studios, music block, lecture theatres etc. were fantastic – a bit like a very small Oxford college. I have to admit that I was quite surprised to be offered a place there. I think the thing that scored most highly on my application was probably my involvement in Sunday school teaching at the church in Dartford, which I had enjoyed so much in the few years prior to applying.

Looking back, the rules at Bishop Otter were almost draconian by today's standards. For instance, meals were taken in the college refectory and had set times. The evening supper was formal – jacket and tie for us boys and dresses for the girls. Nobody could leave until the Principal on the high-table had finished and stood up. If you were late for supper – i.e. after grace had been said – you had to 'bow-in', which meant walking the length of the room down the central aisle and bowing to Miss Murray, the lady Principal. I had to do this on more than one occasion and remember bowing in with an almost musketeer-like flamboyance which was typical of me at this time. Outwardly I was carefree, confident and – being a musician as well as a member of the art department – seen as unfairly talented by some. I suppose, looking back, that it was exactly the sort of impression I wanted to give. Deep down, I was still a rather troubled adolescent.

There was a very approachable chaplain at the college and, having chosen Religious Education as one of my subsidiary teaching subjects, I got to know him very well. It was to him that I took my troubles in the autumn of 1970 – the start of the third and final year. I had been successful throughout the first two years and had managed to pass all the exams but the only section of the course that I really enjoyed was the practical teaching out in schools with real pupils. I had filled the summer holiday auditioning for full-time bands as a professional drummer because I didn't know if I really wanted to continue with my studies. Narrowly missing out on joining one well-known rock band, instead I returned to Chichester for the final year and made arrangements to have a serious talk with the chaplain. I knew that finding my real mother was the problem. Creating an image at college was quite easy, but I realized that even I didn't know who the real me was!

The chaplain, Rev Patterson, let slip that he had been hoping I might come to see him voluntarily. He had noticed things were not right and, even in passing, when he had asked me how things were going he knew my rosy replies were not the truth. Rev Patterson was an astute man and, also being a great listener, he was easy to talk to. I found myself relating the entire story of the search for my mother, starting with the gold watch. I held nothing back and repeated everything that had happened in the Congo exactly as it had been told to me. He got the lot, going right through to the attempts I had made as a child to acquire information on my adoption. I showed him the replies I had received via Colin. I also told him how I had, on more than one occasion, been advised in no uncertain terms to drop the whole thing.

It was relating the missionary story and of my real mother's experiences leading to my existence, that chewed on my emotions. At the time, I didn't know why it should have been so upsetting, but I later realised it was because I had not told the story to anyone for several years: I had bottled it up for a long time. Rev Patterson listened, asked the occasional question, poured me a beer and listened some more. It all came out: I had no blood relatives, all my college friends had brothers, sisters and other family members visiting on a regular basis. Everyone else had extended families going back generations. I had nothing of that.

Who was I and why was everything hidden by such a veil of secrecy? What could I possibly do to find the truth? My adoptive family were wonderful, supportive and loving – I owed them everything BUT it was not the same. Out it came in one great emotional jumble, ending with: 'there you go, that's it'.

Rev Patterson was brilliant. Firstly, he took me seriously and didn't attempt to offer a quick, glib reply. Secondly, and far more important to me at the time, he didn't suggest I drop the whole thing as had happened on previous occasions. He asked for time to think carefully over the whole scenario and to do some research; not into the family itself, but into the legal situation concerning adoption and the rights of those concerned. He asked for my permission to discuss the situation (not the story) with professional friends who may have better specialist knowledge. I agreed of course, and we arranged to meet at a later date, I think a week hence. I left in a far better state of mind, probably because I had confided the entire story to someone whom I wholly respected as a friend and a professional.

Our second meeting was an education for me and prompted the start of my serious research attempts. The first thing he did was to make the point that now, being an adult, the world had to treat me slightly differently. That didn't mean I had a right to all the information I might want, but it did mean that the excuse of me being 'just a child' could no longer be used. At least I should be afforded the respect that any adult should expect. Having said that, the facts he related were daunting: even an adult had no right to adoption information and agencies were under no compulsion to divulge it. I still had no right to a copy of my original birth certificate or any information the agency or home held about my real mother or her family. In the light of his discoveries he was actually quite surprised I knew as much as I did about my birth mother, especially regarding the missionary link with the Congo. Most adoptions in the 1940s, he said, were shrouded in secrecy where adoptive parents and birth mothers never met and even names were not divulged. This was especially true where the child was from a single mother and adopted by two new parents. He also thought that my having seen the two original documents was probably unusual. However, my mother's name was clearly not enough to go on if I wanted to make progress.

This meeting fired me up to get started, and Rev Patterson

ended it by suggesting that I write some letters: one to the Baptist Missionary Society and, more importantly, another to The Haven itself.

In all the years I had been searching, I had never written to The Haven and for one good reason. After getting the 'Master Martyn Bradley' reply from the Baptist Missionary Society, I was very worried that if The Haven received a letter from me, I might receive a similar rebuke AND they might notify my adoptive parents of my communication. I had always resolved not to let Mum and Dad know of my searching and I had, therefore, seen contacting The Haven as a big problem. Would they tell my adoptive parents of my vain attempts? Childish thinking, I know – and it had really never occurred to me as a child that the home would have had little or no chance of tracing Mr and Mrs Bradley after all those years! Now things were different: I had just turned twenty-one and the problem had dissolved.

I wrote to The Haven during the latter part 1970, quoting all the details on my 'Ralph' information sheet. I went into great detail concerning the Wellington story and the reasons I was so desperate to find my birth mother. I probably wrote far too much and I remember agonizing over the wording as if I was trying to make a very special case for them to perhaps break their own rule and furnish me with the information. The letter to the Missionary Society was a much simpler affair and purely requested information as to the protocol for contacting former missionaries who had worked in Leopoldville. I had learned the hard way as a child and was now determined to make my enquiries correctly. I posted these two letters at the central post-office in Chichester, then went to my favourite pub overlooking the Priory Park and had far too many beers.

The reply from the Baptist Missionary Society came quickly and I do remember thinking when I collected it from the college post box, that maybe being an adult had made some difference. I must admit that it was with some trepidation that I slit open the envelope. The response was similar to the reply received so many years earlier but without the previous admonishment. It opened with: 'Dear Mr Bradley, thank-you for your enquiry' and continued in a friendly but business-like manner. The familiar procedure was outlined: members of specific families who wished to contact missionaries who had previously worked for the Society should address correspondence to the certain missionary by name c/o the Baptist Missionary Society, who would then forward the letter. It also added that although they did hold a comprehensive list, it was by no means complete as some missionaries (certainly from so long ago) had not kept in contact with the Society and, of course, some had passed away.

Initially, I was really happy with the reply as it was the first positive, respectful letter on the subject that I had ever received and, for the first time, opened up the real possibility of making contact with the Wellington family. But there was a problem: I actually hadn't a clue what to do with the opportunity. I was by this time twenty-one years old. I had spent years thinking about possible contact, a wonderful reunification of loving mother and long-lost son, but now the possibility renewed all my emotional turmoil and the same old questions raised themselves larger than ever. Also I could only write to the missionary, Dorothy Ruth's father. What could I say after years during which he may have done all he could to forget what would have been one of the worst events in his entire life, if not the very worst. 'Dear Mr Wellington, I'm your daughter's long lost illegitimate son.' ... I don't think so! There had been aspects of the original story which suggested Dorothy Ruth was sent to England to give birth to avoid any scandal. Suppose her mother had made all the arrangements, her father never knew and was under the impression that she had been returned for safety reasons. What on earth could I do without causing him terrible distress?

I took the letter to Rev Patterson to ask his advice, which turned out to be very simple. 'Why don't you write to Mr Wellington and explain that you want to make contact with his daughter. You knew her very well soon after she returned from Africa in 1949.' This was brilliant. As he explained, the Wellington family wouldn't recognise the name Martyn Bradley due to the adoption policy of total secrecy and I'd possibly get an address, finally, for Dorothy Ruth.

Soon after this, and certainly before I wrote the Wellington letter, the reply came through from The Haven. In fact, it was my original letter being returned – the home had closed its doors in early 1969: I was too late.

I wrote the letter to Mr. Wellington c/o the Baptist Missionary Society early in 1971. It took a substantial period of time for me to come to terms with the possible enormity of the path I was taking. I went home to Dartford for the Christmas holidays and anguished over the whole thing. I came very close to confiding in my Mum, but I had kept my activities secret for so many years, that in the end, I remained silent. It was a difficult few months for me and, on several occasions, I put pen to paper only to find my resolve failed at the last moment and I ripped the letters up. The format finally was a simple, informal request to Mr Wellington stating who I was and that I would like to write a letter to his daughter, Dorothy Ruth, who had been a friend in 1949. The letter was addressed to the Baptist Missionary Society in London and sealed. I remember posting it at around midnight after playing a jazz gig at The Smuggler's Roost in Rustington on the coast. Amazing how small details like this have stuck in my mind for so long.

All the months of soul-searching and anguish ended a couple of weeks later when the reply arrived.

There was no Wellington on the list.

Chapter 6
Somerset House

I dealt with the fact that this was probably the end of the road by blanking it from my mind and indulging in all the things I enjoyed most in life. There was seldom a day when 'Ralph Wellington' didn't appear somewhere in my thoughts, but I learnt not to dwell on it.

I qualified from college at the end of June in 1971, went to Guernsey to stay with a girlfriend for a while, and then took the road to the beaches of Devon and Cornwall, set on improving the surfing skills which the time in Guernsey had initiated. Down in the West Country, a seemingly endless summer of sun, waves and girls enabled me to move on and think no more of my quest.

The main activity in life throughout the following years, apart from teaching of course, was music. I had looked for teaching jobs anywhere in the country there was sea and surf, but remained in Chichester due to my being part of a very successful folk band at the time. My beloved drums were in the cupboard for the time being and I had shifted from jazz to immersion in the world of folk music. I had become a well-known guitarist in the area and had also taken up the concertina as a melody instrument.

Throughout this part of the early 70s, I made regular visits back to the family home in Dartford. Although I had decided to plant roots firmly in Sussex, my adoptive parents were very important to me, and seeing them was always a joyous occasion. They were responsible for giving me not only such a wonderful childhood but the love, guidance and values upon which my life had flourished.

In 1973, Mum died suddenly from a heart attack. I was in my rather unwholesome flat just outside Chichester at the time and, fortuitously, Dave Chandler from Dartford was staying with me. Without his consolation and presence, I'm not sure what I would have done. I was dreadfully sad, but I suddenly felt guilt that I had spent so much time thinking about my birth mother. Had I neglected Mum, who had given me so much? All my research, for so long a secret, now felt a deception. She'd given me everything and I'd repaid poorly. It was only after she died that I realised just how much I had loved her.

By 1975, I had a great job at the local High School for girls and was supplementing my income with gigs on the folk circuit and at the wide variety of large holiday establishments that adorned the coastline from Brighton to Portsmouth. Just occasionally, I played up in London. It was on one of these trips that I visited Somerset House on the Strand, the home of all birth, marriage and death records in England. The people at Somerset House were very helpful. I already knew my date of birth, my birth name and the name of my birth mother, so I had no trouble obtaining the birth certificate for Ralph Allan Wellington, at The Haven.

That day, I gained the first piece of new information related to my birth: Dorothy Ruth was listed as being a solicitor's secretary, and there was an address in London under the 'Residence' heading – 27 Howitt Road, Belsize Park, NW3. I didn't know if this was the address of a friend of the Wellington family, the address where Dorothy Ruth stayed after I was born, or possibly both. Could I find out after so much time?

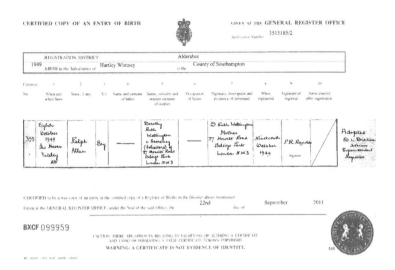

Searches for a Dorothy Ruth Wellington's birth any time around 1933 came out blank. We widened the search years, in case the age of sixteen was not quite correct. Of course, there were no computer files then and I think I'm correct in remembering that the records were all kept on Microfiche, so the researcher who helped me must have been extremely patient. I was surprised and at the same time extremely puzzled. I had hoped at least to get a rough location in the UK via the birth certificate, but there was no birth record for a Dorothy Ruth Wellington at all. The only conclusion we could come to was that she had actually been born out in the Congo, which meant that the family had been there for some time, with no intentions to return to England even after the events of 1949. Maybe Dorothy had been shipped back home to Africa sometime soon after I arrived? Yet more disappointment. Maybe it really was the end of the road. The story had started in Africa and I felt its secrets remained there.

I was resigned to getting nowhere but did write a letter to the house in Belsize Park, addressed to the occupier and asking for any information on the Wellington family who may have lived there in the 1940s. I even enclosed a stamped, addressed envelope. I wasn't surprised when I received no answer. I carried on with my life and it would take another twenty years, and the advent of digital records on the internet, before I committed to any further serious research.

It was during this long period of inactivity that I actually mislaid several documents including the original replies from the Baptist Missionary Society and my original birth certificate copy. I had to reorder this certificate twice more: once in 2003 and again in 2011. I wasn't doing very well!

Chapter 7

Many blessings – Helen and Abi

During all those early years of research, the main obstacles to progress were information and communication. I had suffered from a distinct lack of one, and a naïve inability to effectively use the other. Now I had grown up somewhat, I was in a much better position to take advantage of any further information that might come to light. Unfortunately, none was forthcoming and it was not until both information and communication were revolutionised by the development of the internet that I had the opportunity to seriously take things further. That is not to say that my birth family slipped from my mind. The thoughts were ever-present and I was always frustrated by the inability to do anything of value. The only real development during this long and tiresome period was the passing of the Children Act of 1975. I can best explain the changes this brought by quoting from *The Haven in Yateley* – the history of my birthplace, written by Valerie Kerslake, and published in 2003.

She writes: *The secrecy surrounding adoption stemmed from the first Adoption Act of 1926, when it was intended to protect the two parties from outside interests, not to conceal one from the other.*

Over the years, this evolved into an absolute secrecy that was still accepted in the Adoption Act of 1958, it being thought best for all concerned, that the adopted child's break with his birth family should be total. There had, nevertheless, been talk for several years in favour of access to birth records, but it was only after the 1975 Children Act, that adopted children over eighteen in England and Wales were allowed such access. An additional clause to the Act required those adopted before 1975 to have compulsory counselling before access was permitted. The particular purpose of this was that parents and adopters before that date had every reason to believe that the adopted children would never be able to find out their original names, and unexpected enquiries could well cause alarm and distress, to both the nature parents, and the adopters and their families.

What that meant in a nutshell was that, since 1975, adopted people aged eighteen and over had the right to apply to the Registrar General for the information which would enable them to apply for a copy of their original birth certificate and also to find out which agency had arranged their adoption. This legislation was retrospective, so it meant that anyone who was adopted before 1975 could also apply for a copy of their birth certificate. In other words, if you knew you were adopted, you could use your adopted name to find your adoption order and therefore, your birth mother's name and the location of the birth. That meant you could obtain your original birth certificate.

The passing of the 1975 Act was by no means a 'Eureka' moment for me – I had been in possession of this information since I was twelve. If this absolute secrecy had existed as a matter of course, then how on earth did my adoptive mum have in her possession the documents she had been able to pass on to me thirteen years earlier? Had staff at The Haven passed them on in error or had they come into her possession by more devious means? Was my birth mother a very clever girl who wanted this information to be passed on to the adoptive parents of her child, and found some surreptitious way of achieving it? Was this because she hoped one day I might find her? Had she played some part in the selection process for my new family? From what I had learnt of the adoption system during the 1940s and at The Haven specifically, I was certain the answers to all these questions was a profound NO, but I'm sure you can imagine how my mind was working at the time. I didn't know what to think and many sleepless nights followed. I had received all the information specified in the 1975 Act when I was twelve years old – and without any counselling whatsoever.

Although I got no nearer to the truth for many years, my life developed in a wonderful way and I really could count my blessings.

By 1976, I was firmly established in Chichester, teaching at the Chichester Girls' High School. The folk circuit in those days was huge and early in the year I started my own club, The Sussex Barn, at Fishbourne, a small village just outside Chichester. A success from the word go, it attracted large audiences each week. The music was great fun as I always loved performing; the ambience was wonderful, being held in a traditional Sussex flint barn; but the greatest thing of all was that it was there I met my future wife.

Helen had recently moved to Chichester from London after being appointed as the Speech and Language Therapist at the city's general hospital, and her love of folk music brought her to the club on only the second week of its existence. I got to know her very quickly, naturally, because she was beautiful!

In the June of 1976, I overdid the surfing on the Whit weekend in North Devon and had only been back home for a few hours, when I suffered a spontaneous pneumothorax and my lung collapsed completely – luckily, it was only one of them! I spent five days in the hospital which, of course, gave Helen many opportunities to visit whilst I was captive in my bed. Due to her position on the hospital staff, Helen was not restricted to visiting only during the official hours, which was just as well, as at those times my bed was surrounded by rather a lot of schoolgirls in green uniforms. Helen generally came to see me when she had finished work, still wearing her white coat. This was much to the amusement of the ward sister, who knew perfectly well there was nothing wrong with my speech.

Helen also had a love of the sea and the country so we spent several happy weeks together back in North Devon that summer, surfing, walking, talking, playing music and generally getting to know each other. We married on 22nd October, 1977, and very soon after bought our first home, a small cottage by the sea at Wittering, south of Chichester, where we could even check out the surf from the bedroom window. Life was rosy and the blessings were adding up. Our greatest blessing of all arrived on 3rd May 1983, when our daughter, Abigail Rachel, was born.

Abi's birth changed everything. It is one thing seeing other people's children and babies but nothing prepares you for the pure joy and emotion of seeing your own flesh and blood. Only then did I begin to understand truly what my real mother had gone through in having to give up her child. She was not surrounded by those she loved, but in a foreign land far from home. She must have possessed an inner strength I could not fathom. The desire to find her returned very strongly after Abi was born and I used to talk about it a great deal with Helen, who had known the story from very early in our relationship.

Great opportunities do not crop up too often throughout one's life. If and when they do, one must recognise them and seize the chances they offer. I can remember my adoptive father saying words to this effect many times over the years, especially when I was in my teens.

One of the greatest opportunities for us as a family arose in 1990. At the time I was Head of Careers Guidance at the local Boys' High School and during one rather boring break-time was browsing a slightly out-of-date copy of the *Times Educational Supplement* when I noticed a small advertisement for a 'Careers Teacher Exchange' to Australia. This meant swapping jobs, houses, friends (and even the car!) with an Australian teacher with similar skills – and all paid for by the Commonwealth Exchange League. It sounded too good to be true and at first I thought there would be no chance but after much research and discussion with family and the school, I decided to apply. Following a lengthy selection procedure consisting of interviews, phone-calls and umpteen forms to fill in, I was offered the exchange and the three of us departed for Pambula Beach, New South Wales at the end of 1990.

The journey to Australia was not without its own excitement. It is quite a rare occurrence when one's life is directly affected by serious world events but on this occasion, we came very close. Iraq had invaded Kuwait in August of 1990 and during the weeks prior to our departure from the UK, there had been a massive build-up of coalition troops in Saudi Arabia from America, the UK, Saudi and Egypt. 'Operation Desert Shield' had begun with a view to the liberation of Kuwait and the situation throughout the Middle East was somewhat volatile. Our Cathay Pacific flight's scheduled stopover was in Bahrain and, we subsequently discovered, was one of the last group of planes to stop there before the airlines began to redirect their routes away from the potential war-zone in the Gulf. As we taxied up to the Bahrain airport buildings, white vans screamed out to meet us and the plane was then completely surrounded by Arab guards with machine-guns – more to keep others off the plane than us on it – but still a rather disconcerting experience. We were not allowed to leave the plane but, as it was stiflingly hot and humid, all the doors were opened, affording an even better view of what was happening outside. After what seemed like hours and hours but in reality was rather short of 90 minutes, we continued our journey towards Hong Kong. We left Bahrain much relieved and looking forward to a three-day stopover in the Orient.

The remaining part of the journey to Australia passed as expected. We had been warned of the infamous approach and landing at Hong Kong's Kai Tak airport and this didn't disappoint. It was a truly amazing experience banking through the tower blocks of Kowloon and descending to the runway built on the reclaimed land of Victoria Harbour. Seven-year-old Abi was determined to see this and had managed to stay awake throughout the entire flight. By the time we had slowed to taxi speed at the end of the runway, she was fast asleep.

The three-day break in Hong Kong was a wonderful attack on all the senses, so much so that we made the decision to cut the year short so we could return for an extended stay over Christmas at the end of 1991. Australia was to be our new life, albeit temporary, and we were eager to get there. Yet another Cathay flight took us overnight on the final leg and, once we had recovered from the New Year's Eve party at 35,000 feet, we arrived tired but happy in Sydney on the 1st of January 1991.

The factors influencing the decision to go had been many but one of the most important was the opportunity to see my adoptive father once more. After Mum's death in 1973, he had remarried and, after just a few years, had retired and made the decision to emigrate to New Zealand.

I was still very aware of the blessing he and Mum had been, especially throughout my early life. Helen and I had visited him and his new wife, Betty, several times when Abi was young but it had been over four years since they had left the country for good. An opportunity to see him again on the far side of the world was one not to be missed but did not arise until well into the exchange year. New South Wales operated a four-term year and it was not until the July holiday that we had two whole weeks free from conferences and cultural visits.

I remember very clearly how I became increasingly unsettled and agitated as the New Zealand visit loomed closer. I was really looking forward to seeing Dad again but there was a certain apprehension creeping in. By this time he and Betty had been living for four years in close proximity to Betty's son and his wife and children, a ready-made family as far away as it was physically possible to be. I knew that we would be made to feel extremely welcome but I guess it was that sense of belonging that was again casting the doubt. Mum and Dad had been the central figures in my development for so many years but now, with Mum gone, I had to share Dad with people I'd never met. Maybe I wasn't sure how I would react to meeting this new Bradley family.

We flew into Auckland in July 1991 to clear blue skies after the three-hour flight from Sydney. In England we seem to have this notion that Australia and New Zealand are close, next-door neighbours, whereas in reality they are separated by well over 2000km of ocean – roughly the same distance as London to Casablanca!

Naturally, I had spent much of the flight wondering how Dad and Betty would seem after almost five years. I knew there would be changes but I wasn't really prepared for just how extensive the changes were. Dad met us at the airport and we travelled in his car to Tokoroa near the hot springs of Rotorua. This would be our home for the next two weeks. It was wonderful to see Dad again, and Betty of course. We were made to feel very welcome but it was very soon apparent that they really had aged and changed considerably. The same old sense of humour was there along with the twinkle in my Dad's eye but both he and Betty had put on a great deal of weight and had slowed down physically and mentally.

Looking back over so many years now, I remember a wonderful holiday full of all things New Zealand. Dad, along with Betty and my stepbrother Nick and his family, had organized an interesting series of events for us. We went to the traditional Maori, hangi feast, complete with the raucous Hakka welcome; we explored the hot springs, geysers and boiling mud of the Rotorua area; saw in detail the workings of the North Island forestry commission (for whom Nick was working); saw a great deal of the stunning countryside and were introduced to lots of sheep! In those days, there were three and a half million people and sixty million sheep in NZ, evidently – amazing what one remembers. For the entire two weeks we were spoilt rotten, especially Abi, who, not surprisingly, I remember as being the star of the occasion. Yes, it was a perfect visit but something wasn't right.

Initially I couldn't put my finger on it but the notion kept gnawing away from the moment we arrived and I soon realised that the new feeling I was experiencing was one of worry. I wasn't worried any longer about the family and any concerns about belonging had been erased by the warmth of the welcome we had been given. This was a very specific worry: a worry about change, the aging process and mortality. Dad and Betty were not quite the same people I remembered. They were now in their seventies and not at all fit and well.

I was tempted to tell Dad about the search. I came very close to doing so but in the end decided against it – the visit was wonderful as it was. All the worries were mine alone. My birth mother would now be almost sixty and all my attempts to find her had proved futile. How much time was actually left for this quest? I spent several restless nights trying to cope with the realisation that time does not stand still. I don't think I had actually thought about this before and all the old concerns about my search raised their heads. I really didn't know what I could do. I think I must have bottled up all the frustration. I certainly didn't want to burden Helen with my worries whilst we were having such a great time on the far side of the world.

Our New Zealand visit ended as it had begun, back in Auckland and, having spent two wonderful weeks on the North Island, we returned to Australia. It was an emotional parting. I was happy in the knowledge that life in New Zealand had been exactly the right choice for Dad but knew deep down that this farewell was almost certain to be final.

The exchange year in Australia was a little like the intermission there used to be during a long film at the cinema. A chance to relax from the concentration, make a noise, grab some refreshment and stretch the limbs before settling down again for the second instalment. This intermission was, however, in the middle of life itself but did still afford the same relaxations and we returned to 'the second instalment' feeling generally refreshed, exhilarated and ready to concentrate on part two.

Once we had returned from Australia, things quickly returned to the normality we had enjoyed before the exchange. Abi did very well throughout the rest of her schooling and, having passed all her exams with flying colours, flew the coop for university study in Exeter.

The nineties were a decade during which the family was extremely happy and much of this happiness centred around Abi's achievements. She had finished school with excellent exam passes, together with a Duke of Edinburgh Gold Award, which was presented to her at a garden party at Buckingham Palace. We all attended what was one of life's exceptional days. Perhaps I didn't want to distract her at that time with my emotional upheavals, so it wasn't until she was home during one university vacation, that I related the entire story. I think this was December 2002. That date would certainly fit perfectly with what was to follow.

Chapter 8

Quest renewed

L ike all before her, Abi was amazed by the story. I thought she might be saddened or angered by the fact I had not divulged it earlier in her life, but there was nothing of the sort. She wanted to know everything about the search I had been involved with for so long and why I'd given up. I tried to explain that I hadn't given up but had just found nothing new for years. I went right through the entire thing from the early disappointments at school to the new concerns raised during the visit to New Zealand. I told her I had actually even been using the internet, although it was a rather different beast from the one we have today and still very much in its infancy as far as us mere mortals were concerned. In my opinion at the time, searching was haphazard to say the least and rarely produced good results. Just about all searching was done on Internet Explorer which crashed regularly and seemed so very slow. I had achieved nothing for a very long time. The other problem had been communication – in other words, email. All my emailing in the early 21st century had been via Internet Explorer and again this was unreliable and slow. The email address was provided via the service provider and one could only access the mail on the home PC. I was not a complete internet dinosaur but, compared with Abi's generation, my use of it was limited. I had had internet access from very early on via school, certainly in the 1990s, and the Dorothy Ruth searches had begun almost immediately but to no avail.

I can't remember the exact search criteria I would have used all those years ago, but they would have been something like 'Wellington family missionaries' or 'Wellington missionaries Belgian Congo 1940s' or 'Missionaries in the Belgian Congo'. My most common search was obviously for 'Dorothy Ruth Wellington'. This went on for some time, always with the same result – zero. I was resigned to getting nowhere, despite using the greatest development in communication since the printing press.

I had searched for the 'Baptist Missionary Society' on several occasions and discovered late in 2002 that they had a website. In the light of my previous enquiries, I did not make further contact with them at that time but did keep referring back to their website. It was in early 2003 that, having visited yet again, I noticed the site had changed substantially both in layout and content. The word which hit me straight between the eyes was 'Archives'. Was it worth another contact with them? Maybe they had far more comprehensive information on previous missionaries by this time. Organisations not only had internet access, but they also had all the other facilities that the modern computer allowed, such as databases. Were archives now available to the general public? How far back did they go? Did they have current contact details for families? I was suddenly very excited by the prospects the internet was opening up. This was certainly the future. Maybe I had finally struck gold here in the present! On the website was the usual 'contact us' button. I stared at it endlessly.

After a great deal of mental anguish, mixed with great

excitement, I decided to take one step at a time and sent the following email:

From: Mart
To: Baptist Missionary Society
Sent: 16 January, 2003
Subject: Family trace

Hi there,
I am researching my family tree and need to find records of BMS overseas missions in the late 1940s. I know my family were involved in Africa at that time. Is there a records office or whatever?
Also interested in a home run by the BMS/Baptist Women's League called 'The Haven' in Camberley – same time???
Thanks for any follow-up/leads/ideas you may be able to give me. I've been trying this on and off for about 30 years – no luck yet!!
Cheers
Mart Bradley

In this new world, reply was almost instant and actually arrived the next day.

From: Jenny Lunn
To: 'Mart'
Sent: 17 January, 2003
Subject: RE: Family trace

Dear Mart,
I deal with enquiries from the public about our archives; we don't have a publically-accessible records office. If you

give me the full names of the people you're trying to trace
and what information you want to know about them, I can
look it up for you. Similarly, for what you want to find out
about The Haven. I haven't heard of it, but I can ask
around in a department that might know.
Look forward to hearing back from you.
Jenny Lunn
Executive Assistant to the General Director
Baptist MS World Mission

My response to this was to actually jump up and down in a
state of semi-euphoria. For the first time in almost forty years,
someone was going to help me! I decided to tell Jenny the whole
story.

Hi Jenny,
Thanks so much for your quick reply – only just
discovered your new site – I've been trying to find
information for so many years and a quick reply is great!
It's a long story so you may as well know it all – it's an
interesting one!
The family I am trying to find information about are the
Wellington family who were missionaries in The Congo –
possibly Leopoldville in the late 40s. Specifically,
Dorothy Ruth Wellington aged 16, daughter of the
missionary family. I heard the whole story many times
throughout my life from my adoptive parents – it never
varies! Although details of places had been remembered
rather than written down, the names are exactly correct –
I have been given the original birth and adoption
documents.
The Wellington family were caught up in the trouble
which flared up in late 1948 to early 1949. I understand

there were deaths and violations amongst the missionary people – I don't know whether the Wellingtons suffered casualties. Dorothy Ruth Wellington was one of the prime targets. I have this as occurring in Leopoldville, but, as I say, all this is via word of mouth rather than by written evidence. The Wellingtons left for England (or Dorothy Ruth on her own) in the Autumn of 1949 and Dorothy gave birth to a son – Ralph – at The Haven Home for Mothers and Babies, Vigo Lane, Yateley, Nr Camberley. She was admitted there on arrival by boat at Southampton and gave birth at the home. This was run by the Baptist Union of Great Britain and Ireland (Baptist Women's League). The Gen Secretary is given as Rev M E Aubrey. Ralph was adopted by a Baptist family, the Bradleys, in October 1949, with the date of birth given as 8th October, 1949.

As you can imagine, Jenny, trying to get information when the establishment concerned has long since ceased to exist is proving extremely difficult!! (I was told by letter some years ago it had closed in 1969.) I don't think I want to contact the immediate family concerned after all this time for obvious reasons. I do, however, want to learn as much of the truth as possible.

Thanks for any help at all you can give. Please feel free to ring me if you need further info.

Cheers

Mart Bradley/Ralph Wellington

I can clearly remember feeling extremely strange during the three-day wait for a reply. It was a specific feeling that I can't describe fully in a few sentences. It came and went as I anguished over what the reply would contain. I do, however, remember the realisation of what it was at the time. I was frightened.

Chapter 9
Dead end

Some days in one's life are both monumental and unforgettable. The wedding, the birth of a child and moving into one's first house. 22 January, 2003, would be on the list for me too but for all the wrong reasons. Two days earlier, I was high on expectation but Jenny's reply knocked everything out of me and left me groping for any shred of comfort.

Sent: 22 January, 2003
Subject: Family trace

Dear Mart,
Thank you for that very interesting story. I have researched via the Baptist Missionary Society archive office, but am sad to say that I can find no evidence to support the story happening in the Belgian Congo. There are certainly no reports of any attacks on Missionary families during this period. We hold no records of a Wellington family in our archive, which is now almost complete. They would surely be well-known to the society had they worked during the late 1940s. I am

passing on the details to a colleague whose mother was working in Leopoldville during the 1950s. She may be able to help you.

Sorry I can't do more,

Jenny Lunn

I cried a lot when I read this. It wasn't Jenny's fault. She had been so professional in her replies and had actually helped me, the first ever to do so. However, I didn't have too long to reflect on the contents because the very next day, an email arrived from Jenny's colleague. She had talked at length with her mother, who had been in Leopoldville at the end of the 1940s and throughout the early part of the 1950s. She was naturally very well informed concerning the Congo and the Baptist missionaries who had worked there. The two replies together turned my world on its head. There was no record or knowledge, either from the society or the lady who had lived there for so long, of any Wellington family ever having worked in Leopoldville or, for that matter, any other area of the Belgian Congo. It was also extremely unlikely that any Wellingtons had ever worked for the Baptist Missionary Society at any time.

The whole story was a fabrication. Maybe it had been told to my adoptive parents by someone at The Haven in order to disguise the true reasons for Dorothy Ruth being there. Maybe they had got the initial facts incorrect. I was convinced she couldn't have made it up herself. If it was a total fabrication, then why make it so dreadfully complex with the journey on the boat from Africa, the violations and the secret pregnancy? There had to be elements of truth in it which, like Chinese whispers, had mutated over the early years in the telling. Or maybe elements of the truth had been forgotten during the 1950s. Whatever the cause, the story by the time it got to me never varied. I came to the sad realisation that for forty years, I had been chasing a ghost.

Chapter 10
Eureka moment

Over the next decade, the internet was to develop almost exponentially as we moved into the age of iPhones and tablets. One of the growth areas was in genealogy and many new websites came online promoting the tracing of family members and the building of family trees from one's own living room. This, of course, became the only source of information worth bothering with as quick and easy access to nationwide records of births, marriages, deaths and the ten-year cycle of censuses was becoming the norm. 'Genes reunited.co.uk', 'findmypast.co.uk', 'familysearch.org' and 'ancestry.co.uk' were all online quite early on and it was these sites that I continually found myself surfing. I had been knocked back so hard by the revelations of the Baptist Missionary Society that it took me a long time to try any further research. I had no idea where to go. I would sporadically open one of the sites to do a 'Dorothy Ruth Wellington' search, but I had resigned myself to the inevitable nil return.

It was not an easy time for the family. Abi passed the selection process for the Royal Military Academy Sandhurst, and thus became an officer in the British Army. We were very supportive and proud of her achievements, but the tours of duty in both Iraq and Afghanistan were times of extreme stress for us left behind. The journey to discover my blood relatives was emotional enough and the thought of losing the only blood tie in my life, my wonderful daughter, was simply too much to bear. We carried on with life as best we could.

For Helen, this also meant serious research into her family. By 2010, we were both retired and thoroughly enjoying the extra time and freedom. Helen had become interested in completing as much as possible of her family tree, many of whom came from the area north of York. Searches and enquiries were far more productive than those to which I was addicted, but in order to fully make use of all the National Archives, she took out a subscription to ancestry.co.uk. This site had been on the internet since 2002 and contained some of the largest searchable databases of genealogy information online. Helen made extensive use of the site's facilities and her family knowledge grew greatly. I, in contrast, got no further. Every so often the site would advertise a new feature, with one example being the records from the two world wars, searchable by regiment and unit, which quite suddenly became available. I did use this one to find my adoptive father's record as a radar specialist. We received mildly interesting e-mails informing us of these updates.

By this time I was very disheartened and came as close as I have ever been to giving up completely. Once again, it was Abi who convinced me to keep trying. She, of course, had very few relatives and talked passionately about needing some! If Dorothy Ruth had married and had children, there could be quite a few by this time. I carried on with occasional searches, but really did think it was over. My mother could have been in her late seventies by then and I was past my sixtieth birthday. Could any good really come of it even if there was a contact made after all this time?

. . .

2011 was to be a year of change for us. Firstly, Abi had decided to leave the army and look for pastures new in civvy street. She had enjoyed a two-year posting with the Royal Gurkha Rifles, including a memorable trip to Nepal to work with the Gurkha Welfare Trust, and things weren't going to improve on that. Deep down, we were rather glad of this. Had she remained, she would almost certainly have given another tour of duty overseas in the near future.

Music was still very important in my life, but playing gigs at pubs and clubs until the early hours of the morning was becoming less of a pull and I decided to quit 'Power of 3', the great blues and rock band I had been a member of for so many enjoyable years. Golf and the garden were keeping me happy and filling much of my time. Helen was now fully retired, a member of more than one choir, and thoroughly enjoying her singing activities. I lived in a beautiful house with a beautiful garden in a quintessentially English village. How easy it would be to accept this in perpetuity!

In September of 2011, yet another e-mail dropped in from ancestry.co.uk. New that month, in their Immigration and Travel Section, they announced the addition of the complete UK incoming passenger lists from 1878 to 1960. I had already tried searches for immigration in the 1940s and received the usual result. It was quite late on a wet, autumn evening that Helen logged me into her Ancestry account once again. She left me to it and I finally found the relevant section. The boxes to fill in were many and quite specific and I completed the few sections for which I had any information: names – no problem; arrival date – no idea, but 1949 sometime; sailing from – no idea, but Africa somewhere; port of arrival – possibly Southampton. I put this all in anyway. I'd filled in so many of these various search forms and I was starting to get the same gnawing feeling – this wasn't looking too hopeful. I hit the search button.

My initial response was the shock of total disbelief when I saw what immediately popped up on the screen.

Name: Dorothy Ruth Wellington
  Birth: *Blank*
  Departure: *Blank*
  Arrival: Date: 1949 – Southampton, England. Total records: 1

At last! A 'eureka' moment.

For a while I could do no more than stare at the computer screen and it was some time until I managed to hit 'view record'. What then appeared was a photograph of the most important piece of paper I had seen since Mum gave me the two certificates back in 1961. It was a single page from the record of passengers who had travelled to England on the Union Castle Steamship company's *Capetown Castle* from the South Africa ports. Dorothy Ruth's entry was one of seven passengers listed as having travelled from Port Elizabeth in South Africa. A long way from the Belgian Congo!

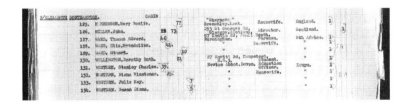

The second bombshell of this entire story, which now had spanned six decades, was to be found typed into the 'Proposed address in the United Kingdom' column: 27 Howitt Rd, Hampstead N.W.3. Exactly the same as that on my original Ralph Wellington birth certificate.

'Helen, I've found her! Can you believe it, I've actually found her, and she really did come from Africa!' It was then that I was overcome by the emotions of the moment and burst into tears. I had found my Lady of Shalott.

I cannot adequately describe the feeling I had following the revelations of that day. Words fail me and it is only at moments like these that one really encounters one's failings. After all the years of wondering, surmising, even doubting, the Lady of Shalott had reached the shore. I thought back to the little boy staring at the painting. Even in his childlike way, he knew the lady in the boat held the key.

Once the initial shock and extreme happiness had returned to a semblance of normality, I started to think carefully about the issues the discovery raised. The matching address left no doubt that this girl was my mother. She had been twenty-one – not sixteen. She left from Port Elizabeth in January and arrived in England on the 11th February 1949, and could only have been about a month into her pregnancy – would she have known? The origin of the voyage was South Africa; the Congo was the cruelest part of the fabrication and had caused me so much anguish.

I was over the moon at my discovery but realised that whilst I was close I still had no evidence of Dorothy Ruth's family in either hemisphere. Who was she? Why had she really come to England? What was the missionary part of the story? Was there any other family? Was any of it actually true (apart from the wonderful ship)? So many questions.

I needed to come down to earth and get going finding the answers.

Chapter 11
My grandfather's face

Assumption is the mother of all failures. There are numerous versions of this quote but the meaning is always the same. I had been thwarted throughout my search for Dorothy Ruth and, without exception, each instance was because I had assumed. I had assumed the Wellington family must be Baptist missionaries because I was born in a Baptist missionary home. I had also assumed the Congo location of the story was true without investigating any other possibilities. Research throughout the 60s and 70s had been very difficult, but my assumptions had hindered what was already so hard. This time I vowed not to assume anything. Mother sailed from Port Elizabeth – that did not mean the family lived there. I was close, I knew, but I needed to tread carefully.

I was very used to getting nil responses to searches, but the internet was still growing, and more and more information was becoming available. It was quite soon after I directed my research to South Africa that I got a positive hit. The site '1820settlers.com' was building an accurate record of all the families who left England for South Africa in 1820. It was a large site and had a comprehensive search facility. I had been searching for 'Dorothy Ruth Wellington South Africa,' and this one website appeared. Reading further, I discovered that in the early 1800s there was much unemployment in England following the Napoleonic wars and the government encouraged men of working age and their families to emigrate to the Cape Colony. The first of these settlers arrived on 17 March 1820 and were sent to Algoa Bay, Port Elizabeth. Immigrants were needed to populate the frontier area of the Eastern Cape in order to raise the percentage of English speakers and to defend the frontier against the Xhosa people. Many were granted land rights and given land for farms around the Port Elizabeth and Grahamstown areas. Further reading and research on the website showed that one side of the Wellington family tree – my possible grandmother's side – traced back to ancestors who had arrived in Algoa Bay on 15 May 1820. Wow, this was becoming increasingly interesting but also highlighted my ignorance of South African history. Apart from triangular postage stamps and a little about the Boer War and the dreadful apartheid system, I knew nothing.

I really was getting very excited, and the new website accelerated this. Once into 1820settlers.com, another wonderful thing happened. Not only was Dorothy Ruth there, but also the entire Wellington family, her father and mother, her brothers and her husband and children.

'Helen! I've got two sisters, I can't believe it, I've got two sisters!'

As I read further, I was almost shaking – it couldn't all be coincidence – her father was a minister and her eldest brother's name was Ralph. It is difficult to explain how I felt. There in front of me was, very probably, the family I had been trying to find for so long, and yet, there was no proof this was the RIGHT Wellington family, for there was no evidence to connect them with the girl on the ship. It was very likely so because of the name and the location, but this time I was assuming nothing.

Still, this was a very emotional day and I was really enjoying myself by now.

There was nothing else on the internet about Dorothy Ruth so I turned my attentions to her father Abraham Arthur, and searched him together with 'Healtown', the mission school mentioned on 1820settlers.com at which he had been the Governor. I was surprised that very little appeared. The most interesting thing was that one or two entries mentioned Nelson Mandela. Reading one site, I realised the school's name had been incorrectly spelt on 1820settlers.com, and should have read – Healdtown. My search engine didn't correct errors or make suggestions in those days; it just did what it was told. I corrected the spelling on my Abraham Arthur Wellington search and it returned not just a handful of results – I could now choose between several thousand!

It was totally incredible reading of Arthur Wellington, possibly my grandfather. The Haven story was correct in part – he was an ordained minister and he was a missionary in that he was the Governor of Healdtown, the Methodist Mission station whose high school was attended by Nelson Mandela. Oh my, it must be true, this must be my family. As I read further, it became apparent that Arthur Wellington was a great man. Could I really be part of a family such as this? I began to experience that strange feeling of nervous fear creeping in. What I needed to find out more than anything else at that point, and the question I kept asking myself, was: what do they look like?

One of the items flagged up on the Wellington/Healdtown search was a report of a new picture coming to light taken at Healdtown during Mandela's time there. It showed the school staff with Arthur Wellington in the centre of the front row, with Nelson Mandela standing with the other students. Unfortunately there was a large crack across the original picture, going right through Arthur Wellington's face, so it was not much help at all. I decided to write an e-mail to the Nelson Mandela Foundation, explaining who I was, or thought I was, and outlining why I desperately needed a picture of Arthur Wellington. This, I vividly remember, I sent very late at night after a long and emotionally draining internet session.

The following lunchtime, there was an e-mail back from an extremely helpful researcher at the foundation. She wished me luck, and attached the portrait photograph of Arthur Wellington from his time at Healdtown. Things had happened so quickly over the previous day or so, especially when compared with the span of time since the search began, that I was in a whirl. What could possibly happen next?

I clicked to open the picture, and stared, transfixed. Now I knew I had found my birth family at last. I recognised myself in the face of my grandfather.

It is actually quite a difficult task to accurately describe what I was feeling at that precise moment. Certainly there were facial features which I instantly could relate to: the set of the chin, the deep lines joining the nose to the edges of the mouth, and especially the nose itself, but I was by no means looking at myself, two generations removed. However, I knew.

I was at peace for the first time in what seemed a positive age of uncertainty. I sat quietly for some time.

'Wow,' I whispered. Then, 'Come and look at this, Helen.'

My wife and I stared together at Arthur Wellington, and she could see the quiet elation his image had produced in me. I suddenly realised the root of this peaceful contentment: this was the first blood relative I had ever seen. Not only did I now know who he was; with him at the head of the family tree, I finally knew who I was.

This sounds as if it should have represented the end of a very lengthy quest and a reason to celebrate. In fact it was the start of the most difficult of situations, and by far the most emotional few days of the entire fifty-year search. I felt elated. I didn't need to make any assumptions anymore, and had in front of me the whole recent family tree of the girl I had so needed to find. There lay the problem. This was no longer an idea, a dream, a desire. This was now a reality, and it was a reality that could do untold damage if handled in the wrong way. My mother had been married since 1951 and had two daughters who would now be just a few years younger than myself. They both had children themselves. I had established that Grandfather had died in 1944, so nothing was going to trouble him, but how many of these people, if any, knew of my existence? I talked the whole thing over with Helen for a long, long time, and emailed Abi to give her the news, attaching Arthur Wellington's picture. Abi was, as we all were, very excited, but could see the nature of the choices I had to make. I had done all I had set out to do – I had found the Lady of Shalott.

One of the biggest decisions of my life now loomed.

Chapter 12
Contact

The decision of whether to make contact was only an option at this time due to the fact that there was an email address on the Wellington pages within the 1820settlers.com website, the address of Stefan Hrabar, the person who had supplied the family details. Whilst there was much Wellington family information available, there were no contact details and no residential addresses. I had no idea who Stefan Hrabar was, and he didn't appear in the Wellington family tree on the site. Whilst decision-making has not always been the strongest facet of my personality, I was determined not to get this one wrong, and thought about the possible repercussions for many hours before I acted. The reality of the situation was daunting. I had spent a lifetime searching for these people, and now I was potentially in a position to cause them anguish and pain. I talked it over at length with Helen, escaped to the golf course as a delaying tactic, but knew that ultimately it was my decision and it had to made one way or another. I was well aware from my research over the years how horrendous situations could become when skeletons suddenly appeared from remote family cupboards, so I was determined to handle the situation with extreme care. The stigmas of the 1950s had changed over the years, but attitudes could still be difficult. Finally, I calculated that I could at least find out who this Stefan was without causing any grief. Treading very carefully, and after hours of indecision, I wrote a short informal email to introduce myself.

From: Mart Bradley
To: Stefan Hrabar
Sent: 17 September, 2011
Subject: Wellington family research

Hi Stefan,
I've just spent hours poring over the Wellington family information on the 1820settlers website and I've noticed most of it was posted by you – an amazing job!
Are you related yourself? If so, where do you fit in?
Abraham Arthur Wellington was my grandfather.
I have a lot of info to share with you but need to know you are still on this email before I write loads that won't arrive.
Cheers
Ralph

I hit 'send' and sent a silent prayer skywards. I actually had no idea whether I would receive any reply to this. The website had been online for some time, and the email address was not necessarily current. Oh, so many ifs and buts. I started having doubts about the possible enormity of what I'd done. What if he's a friend of Dorothy Ruth – could be a problem but could keep it from going any further. What if he's a friend of Dorothy Ruth's children... I'd signed off 'Ralph', but the email was from Martyn – how clever was this guy? No going back now, even from this one short email.

The reply came back that same day after just a few hours. It took a lot of courage to open it.

> Dear Ralph, I am boarding a flight to Namibia but will be back next Sunday. My brother-in-law is (was) married to Diane Wellington. Please keep in touch.
> Steve Hrabar

I was so relieved to read this. Although the message was brief, it allayed my fears and put him in context with the Wellington family. I knew from my study of the website that Diane Wellington was the daughter of Oswald Frank, one of my mother's elder brothers. Diane was my first cousin... wow... this was becoming just amazing. There was no turning back now. Steve Hrabar was far enough removed to trust with my information. I had a week to decide how much to tell him.

It was during this week that I returned to my UK research, based on what I had discovered on the 1820settlers site. It was very strange. I now knew my mother had married a Philip Jackson. I wondered if the marriage had taken place here or after she returned to South Africa, as I now know she had. I logged into ancestry.co.uk, entered Philip Jackson into the 'Marriages' search, and up it came. This was strange, as when I searched for Dorothy Wellington in the same search engine it came up with nothing – the internet is not infallible. (As I write this, I have tried the search again – it's still a nil return!)

Dorothy married Philip Jackson in 1951 in Oxford. I had no idea when they returned to South Africa.

The decision of what to send to Steve Hrabar was easy in the end. He just sounded like a nice, ordinary guy, so, having come so far already, I decided to send him the lot. I certainly do not intend to reproduce all the emails in their entirety, but I feel it is important that I quote most of this first lengthy email sent to South Africa. It explains the nature of my thinking at the time.

From: Mart Bradley
To: Stefan Hrabar
Sent: 29 September, 2011

Hi Steve,

Hope the trip to Namibia went well. Difficult to know where to start, as you are the first relative, albeit distant, that I have made contact with!! But here goes...

I see your link is via Diane Wellington, whose father, Oswald Frank Wellington, was my mother's brother – both children of Abraham Arthur Wellington – my grandfather and Governor of Healdtown.

Dorothy Ruth Wellington is my mother, and I was born Ralph Allan Wellington on 8th October 1949. I do not appear on any family trees and, after much research, I'm sure the family descendants have no knowledge of my existence. I was almost certainly named after her elder brother Lancelot Ralph.

Dorothy travelled to Southampton England from Port Elizabeth on the *Capetown Castle*, arriving in Feb 1949, and gave birth to me at The Haven Missionary Home for Mothers and Babies in Aldershot district. Following their strict rules, I was adopted immediately and there was no further contact between any of the parties concerned.

The story I learnt as a teenager from my adoptive parents was that my mother was the daughter of missionaries in Africa, had conceived and been sent away from home to have the child in secret – to quote from The Haven history literature that I have (2003), 'It will be hard for younger people today to have any idea of the immense and lasting shame of having a child outside of marriage, forty or fifty years ago. The whole family was deeply disgraced. Parents might feel they had to resign from church or other public duties, and time did not always bring forgiveness.'

This would all ring true if Arthur Wellington had still been alive in 1949. I cannot see Dorothy actually being sent to England by her mother or brothers, and also the length of time between her getting on the boat in Port Elizabeth and my birth is too long. Hence my belief that Dorothy alone knew her situation and got herself away before anyone else found out!! Or – she was coming to England for a totally different reason – as a student (from info on passenger list) and had a relationship sometime immediately before she left SA.

It is only after the incoming migrant passenger lists were added to genealogy sites that I had any breakthrough in my research as I had been told the missionary family were in the Belgian Congo and all enquiries there over many years ended in a blank. Also, I thought the missionary family had been abroad for a much shorter time and didn't realise my mother had been born overseas – hence no birth records for Dorothy Ruth Wellington in the UK! The Wellington family were huge in the Truro area of Cornwall. I have spent a long time researching the family there and also Abraham Arthur's life – most of which you have details of. I have the certificate for his joining the army during the Boer War in 1901 – Somerset East Town Guard – and have researched his time in Healdtown extensively with the help of the Nelson Mandela Foundation. The researchers there have been brilliant and have provided me with the only pictures I have of my grandfather – the resemblance is amazing!! I have enclosed two pictures which you may not have seen. A portrait from the Centenary booklet on Healdtown produced in 1955, and a recently discovered picture of

Healdtown school in 1937. Grandfather is centre 2nd row and back 5th from right is Nelson Mandela.

As you can imagine, all this could come as a bit of a surprise to put it mildly, especially to my mother's immediate family, and I have no desire to make contact, make them aware of my existence or to cause any grief to them. I see on the 1820settlers site that dates of birth and death are only added when a family member is deceased, so I'm assuming Dorothy is still alive – the secret can remain ours for the present. I have the marriage cert of her joining Philip Jackson in 1951, and beyond that there are no records in the UK for the birth of her two daughters, so I assume they went overseas.

I send you this as I'm so impressed with your work on the site and your great interest in the Wellington family – also I guess you're far enough removed to view it in an impartial way!! I'd obviously enjoy your thoughts, comments, etc. – it's a good story!! – any info or help you could give would be appreciated...

Sending this email was, I thought, possibly the end of the entire adventure, because an adventure was exactly what it had been, the adventure of a lifetime. I felt happy that I had managed to pass on the whole story to Steve Hrabar, but at the same time strangely sad that it might well be the end of the road. I'd left the whole thing with him, and would wait to see what he advised. He had contact with the family and would have his own ideas about their possible or probable response.

The reply came back the same afternoon and the content was so unexpected. I was really not contemplating this, but the deed had already been done – the entire story had been sent to Diane, my cousin.

From: Stefan Hrabar
To: Mart Bradley
Sent: 29 September, 2011

Dear Ralph,
Thank you very much for this. Where are you located?
I have passed on your e-mail to Diane Wellington and her daughter Colleen, who is also keen on the family. I have photographs of the Wellington family and other documents. I can get them on to a CD for you. The research for the site on the Wellingtons was prompted by Diane, who gave me a pencil-drawn family tree the size of a double bed. By the way, Diane now lives in the USA. She will know what to do now for the best.

I stared in amazement at the screen for some time. When things got moving with the new internet technology, they really did move quickly. My entire story was now with my first cousin in America, and yet a couple of weeks earlier I had known absolutely nothing.

Chapter 13
The end and the beginning

I had now reached a totally different phase in the development of the search: contact had been made with the immediate Wellington family with all my information and documentation being sent to my first cousin, Diane. Throughout those few days at the end of September and the beginning of October 2011, I was in a state of extreme agitation. I couldn't concentrate on anything for more than a few minutes, played awful golf and was probably not very easy to live with! Helen was supportive, as always, and was almost as excited and amazed as I. She had been with me through years of uncertainty and was very astute. She knew the possible pitfalls that lay ahead. I knew not what the next email would contain: something positive, a wary acceptance, or total rejection.

Diane's email arrived on the 2nd October. I read the first paragraph and started weeping with pleasure.

Dear Ralph,
Since receiving the e-mail sent via Rusty and Steve
Hrabar, I have thought about nothing else. I am amazed,
saddened and at the same time happy to know I have

another first cousin, and in England. I am really looking
forward to meeting you and would like to welcome you
with open arms to the family...

The rest of the email, which was quite long, went on to
describe many events in the family history, speculation as to why
they had occurred and, very interestingly, who my father may
have been. This was a question I hadn't given much time to in the
past, as the original story gave no reason to suggest it would ever
be possible to find out. Now, of course, it widened the detective
work even further.

Here, from Diane, was a communication that was not just
speculation, it also contained answers to many of the questions I
had agonised over for so many years. Most important of these was
that my mother had died around 2002. I cried a lot when I read
this. For so many years I had hoped, prayed, I would meet her one
day. I had had dreams of open arms and banquets for the prodigal
son. I was also angry with myself for not finding her in time. I had
had the answer in that damn ship! Why did I not research via the
shipping companies from Africa, find the main ones, badger them
to see the lists for 1949? I tormented myself for my own stupidity.
The answer really had been in the painting all that time.

I learned many other previously unknown facts from Diane.
(I wrote these down at the time and studied them a great deal.)

- Mother had more than likely told nobody about my
  existence, I was the secret I had always imagined.
  (Possibly told someone after her husband died?)

- Her husband, Philip, had also passed away, before
  mother.

- She had been engaged to a man (let us call him

'Luke'), possibly my father – this was truly amazing food for thought!

- The Wellingtons are a highly educated, successful, close and loving family.

- Mother was amazing – prominent businesswoman, Rotary chair, etc.

- Both my Sisters are alive and well and living still in South Africa – Port Elizabeth.

So much information had come my way during the last few days that I was in danger of being overwhelmed mentally and emotionally. Diane's email was far more than I had ever hoped for as far as a first contact was concerned. One sentence which brought a lump to the throat and had me back in fantasy land was:

'In my heart of hearts, I know that my father did not know about you: he was an upright, hardworking, honest and fair man and he would have done everything in his power to get you back to South Africa and he would have brought you up himself.'

Diane had replied to what was quite an abridged version of my story, as told in the email which was forwarded to her by Steve Hrabar, so the next day, 3rd October, I replied with the whole story from the gold watch to the present day. I had written this so many times by then that it was a joyous and easy task. What was not so easy was composing the one paragraph which I hoped might lead me forward to meeting my two sisters. Since Mother had passed away, this was now priority number one. Diane's letter had been the catalyst for a fundamental change in my mindset. Gone were the ideas I had expressed to Steve Hrabar about not wanting to necessarily make contact: this was now a fundamental desire burning inside me. I thought about that gold watch episode so long ago. I didn't belong. I wasn't a blood relative. Now I had all the knowledge passed on by Diane, I wanted so much to belong. I wanted to be a Wellington. I wrote:

> The thought that I now have a real family hasn't sunk in yet. You mention Ruth's two daughters. How do you think they will respond to a new brother appearing after all this time? Were they aware of the birth I wonder, or was it all kept secret? I would love to contact them. I am desperate to get hold of some family pictures, especially of Ruth as she was around the time she had me. I am so happy but still feel very much in the dark in some respects. I guess it is all a little easier now that Ruth's generation are, sadly, all passed on. I wonder how they would have reacted! What are your thoughts, Diane, on the best way to go about any contact with Ruth's daughters? The thought of two real sisters is wonderful but, having said that, the last thing I would want to do is to upset anyone, especially with such an old skeleton in the cupboard!

Diane replied almost immediately. She was wonderful, and had been busy contacting various Wellington family members with news of the prodigal.

> I am also emotional and know exactly how you feel right now; believe me I am sharing in your excitement and your happiness, but I also feel an inner turmoil.
> I hope you do not mind but I have decided to forward your emails to Stefan Hrabar so he can update the family tree; to my late brother's wife Penny Wellington living in Pretoria, because she is closest to our Uncle Ralph's children; and to cousin Arthur Wellington with the request that he be the go between and be the introduction

to your sisters Fiona and Heather. He is Uncle Ralph's oldest son and I am sure well situated to start the process with Fiona and Heather, as he knows them better than I do. I can only hope that the introduction is one of happiness and acceptance on their part...

So Diane wrote to cousin Arthur Wellington, copying the email to me, and enclosing all my emails, documentation, family photographs and story.

Arthur's return email to me arrived the same day, 4th October. It contained much Wellington family information and another welcome to the family. This was truly wonderful, but my mind was in a state of confusion – great joy at the extended family welcome but so dreadfully worried at the effect the whole scenario would be having on my sisters. The email also included the following, which I think caused me more stress and anguish than I had experienced at any other time in my life:

Hi Ralph,
I am the eldest of the Wellington next generation (of your generation, in fact). I have received all your data and passed all the info on to Fiona, Ruth's eldest daughter, and I have discussed the findings with her. She will be discussing this all with Heather tomorrow, and no doubt, once they have had the opportunity to discuss the matter fully, she will contact you...

This was it; no turning back now.

I often think about that day in 1962 when my adoptive mother sat me down to tell me a story. It was a story that was to dominate my life for the next fifty years. It was wonderful in many ways but very often caused a passion and emotion strong enough to disrupt all the other facets of life. On this day, it was certainly at the peak of its power. I had, after such a long, long time travelling what had seemed at times such a perilous journey, come to the great divide, and the route I would take was now in the hands of those I most longed to be a part of. My sisters knew they had a brother!

I don't remember much about the following day and a half: it was purgatory! Was I being punished for daring to seek the truth?

I do remember spending much of a very sleepless night with the various possible responses competing for my troubled brain's attention. I tried to be objective and consider things from Fiona and Heather's perspective: For me this current situation was the culmination of years of searching. I had always known there was a family there somewhere. For my sisters, this would come as a bolt from the blue. A sudden telephone call that would surely turn their world upside down. I was now absolutely certain that they had no knowledge of my existence at all. After so many years as just the two of them, would there be any room in their lives and their hearts for a brother? I think in the end I fell asleep purely from exhaustion.

I was in no better state the following morning and rushed to the computer the minute I got up. The rest of the day continued very much in the same vein as the previous – mental chaos. I mooched around filling the time with life's mundane jobs: clear up some leaves, check email, run through a new concertina tune, check email, clean the golf clubs, check email: my concentration span was at zero.

The terrible hours of waiting ended late in the afternoon when the email from South Africa arrived. For a while I simply stared at the screen. The subject read – From Fiona and Heather. This was it, the rest of my life was to be revealed by one click of the mouse. Battling to overcome my emotions – an intense mixture of fear, trepidation and anticipation – I hit 'open'.

Chapter 14
Fiona – The phone call

The phone was ringing. I was busy cooking, so I wiped my hands and hurried out of the kitchen, never suspecting that this call, or rather the one that would immediately follow it, would be life-changing in ways I never could have imagined.

It was an ordinary, quiet morning on our farm in the Karoo. Rob and I had lived here, 2½ hours' drive inland from Port Elizabeth, ever since we married in 1979. I loved it. I loved the vast dry wildness of South Africa's open veld, sparsely dotted with sheep and reaching to the far hills. I loved the isolation, the fact that we could stand on our veranda with nothing but the greys, greens and browns of the semi-desert slopes stretching out in front of us.

It was school holidays, and I was enjoying being quietly at home. The various little bits of part-time teaching that I usually do, two days a week, were in recess. I had just finished preparing a whole lot of lesson materials for the coming term – very fortunately, as things turned out – and thinking of this made me satisfied and happy.

I got to the bedroom and picked up the phone. My cousin

Arthur Wellington, my Uncle Ralph's eldest son and the first-born of all the Wellington cousins, was calling from his home in Cape Town. After saying hello, he asked, 'Is Rob there? Can I have a word with him?'

I explained that Rob was out in the veld but would be home for lunch. We went on talking for some time, chatting about the farm and the family – the sheep and the kids – but Arthur never said what it was that he had wanted to talk to Rob about. In between telling him about what each of our children was up to, and enquiring about his also-grown-up offspring, I wondered what it could be.

We said our friendly goodbyes, and rang off. I was on my way back to the kitchen when the phone rang once more. I was surprised to hear Arthur's voice again.

'If Rob isn't there, I'll tell you,' he said, sounding perhaps a little wary.

Intrigued, I encouraged him to continue, wondering what he could be wanting to tell me that he thought he ought first to tell Rob. He cleared his throat, and began. Someone from England had contacted the Wellington family via e-mail, through our cousin Diane in the States. This person in England – here Arthur hesitated and seemed to take a deep breath before he went on – this person in England was related to us, a new and previously unknown relative. I listened, my eyebrows raised. Arthur hesitated again before continuing. 'It seems that... well, it seems that you and Fevvy have a brother, a half-brother!'

'A brother!' I exclaimed in disbelief, my voice rising at least an octave. This was impossible. Ridiculous! The thought flashed through my mind that my Dad was from England. Immediately I dismissed the idea with contempt, for anyone who had known Dad would agree that he had been an innocent, romantic soul, an idealist, not the sort of person to have fathered a child before he met my mom.

Arthur went on. 'His name is Ralph Allan Wellington. He was born in 1949 and is sixty-two years old. He has been looking for his real family for fifty years.'

I was confused, thinking immediately of my Uncle Ralph, my mother's brother, Arthur's father. How could a child of Uncle Ralph's be my brother?

But Arthur was still speaking. 'His mother's name is given on his birth certificate as Dorothy Ruth Wellington.'

I gasped. Ma! Our Ma? No, no, surely not! Arthur explained that this man had been born in a home called The Haven, in England, born there to our mother and given up for adoption. I protested vehemently that this was impossible. My mother had been a very friendly, open person, who had always confided in us, and I was sure that she had told us everything about her life that there was to know. I protested again that she would have told us if something so momentous had happened to her. This just could not be so, I said, and I would require proper proof, like DNA tests, before taking anything like this seriously.

In fact I was so sceptical and suspicious, and so confident that this person in England was either sadly deluded or wickedly scheming, that I chuckled scornfully, 'I'm SURE there is someone in England who thinks he is my brother!' But even as I was speaking, it occurred to me that Ma had in fact been in England in 1949, while she was still single, before she met my Dad there. I admitted this to Arthur, still protesting that for her to have had a child overseas was nevertheless impossible. After all, my sister and I knew all about Ma's three years in England, everything that had happened to her there. She had told us all about it. We had her photo albums and her letter-diary – the carbon copies of the letters she wrote home to her mother.

Chuckling in his turn at my scepticism, Arthur wisely said that he would forward to me all the documents and photographs that he had received from Diane via e-mail, and I could decide for myself. So we said our second goodbyes of the morning, this time with me shaking my head in total disbelief.

I had taken the call on the phone next to our bed, on Rob's side – he usually did all his phoning lying down, to rest his often painful back. Now I sat down on the bed, staring out of the window feeling completely bemused, seeing nothing of the lovely view that I woke up to every day, the view of our green lawn and the vast dry Karoo veld beyond it. What a weird conversation! Of course it was totally impossible that this man's claims could be true. Ma had told us everything about her life. I wondered what to do, and found myself instinctively reaching for the phone again to call my sister. Of course I must tell Fevvy (the family nickname for Heather), even though this bizarre claim would obviously turn out to be nonsense.

Usually on a weekday morning I would dial her number at the school in Port Elizabeth where she was bursar, but now, it being school holidays, I called her at home. She was amazed and stunned at what I was telling her, and just as sceptical as I was. This couldn't have happened to our mother. We talked for quite a while, agreeing that we would wait until we had seen the e-mails before taking any of this craziness seriously.

I wandered about our big old stone farmhouse rather aimlessly after that, still shaking my head every now and again, unable to do anything beyond checking on the food and going to the farm office often to check for new e-mails. Each time there was nothing.

I'd been preparing a variety of meals for Rob because I would be away for the next three days. During term time I usually went to Graaff-Reinet – a 1½ hour drive further inland – every Monday, to teach violin to a handful of pupils and to do my shopping. Now that it was school holidays I was planning to accompany one of my violin pupils to Port Elizabeth, where he would take part in a Youth Orchestra Workshop. We would make the journey early tomorrow morning, and would be staying with my sister. I was looking forward to spending some time with her. My goodness, would we now have something to talk about!

Our mother had brought us up to believe that one should save oneself for marriage, and that was what I assumed she had done herself. She had been devoted to our Dad in all their fifty-one years together, until he died in 2002. She had outlived him by little more than a year. Of course she couldn't have had an illegitimate son, it just didn't fit her character. I found myself muttering the words 'Impossible!' and 'Ridiculous!' as I alternatively checked on the stove and our frustratingly silent computer.

At last, after what felt like an hour, the screen told me that new messages were downloading.

The first thing to come in was an e-mail from our cousin Diane, to Arthur. Diane was just a few years older than me, and I remembered her well from when we were young, before she married and emigrated to America. I looked at the date on her letter – 4th October 2011. This very morning! My goodness. I read her words with increasing amazement as I realised that she seemed pretty convinced of this fellow's claims. By the time I got to the last line, my eyebrows were up in the middle of my forehead:

'The tricky part will be explaining him to Fiona and Heather, and I would ask you to be the go between.'

Well!

Then a second e-mail came in, a string of e-mails and attachments. First was a long letter from Diane to this Ralph-person, dated two days ago. I read it with increasing amazement:

Since receiving the email sent via Steve Hrabar, I have thought about nothing else. I am amazed, saddened, and at the same time happy to know I have another first cousin and in England. I am really looking forward to meeting you and would like to welcome you with open arms to the family.

I only knew your Mother as my Aunty Ruth and was very fond of her. She ran a very successful printing business in Port Elizabeth and raised 2 daughters, Fiona and Heather. She loved my Dad and the families spent many Xmases etc. together. [...]

Perhaps a rosy future awaits you, where you can meet your sisters Fiona and Heather. I am sorry to tell you Ruth died of complications from emphysema in about 2002, but I will have to check when. Phil was already dead and Ruth was in a nursing home in the end but well-tended and visited by Heather, living close to her in Port Elizabeth. Fiona, a high school math and science teacher, married a farmer in the Eastern Province (a Hobson), and I think still teaches in a school close to the farm. Heather married a businessman who eventually bought Ruth's printing firm.

Ruth was a tall very attractive blonde with a large outgoing personality, very well educated and well-spoken and a prominent businesswoman in Port Elizabeth, a church-going Methodist and a humanitarian in her community. What would prompt a woman of her strength of character to do what she did? It does not make sense. Let me tell you my thoughts. I may be wrong, because know I am in the world of conjecture. Ruth was engaged to a builder, -- --, when she left for England. The story I am told is that Ruth met Phil on the boat coming back from England and 'Luke' was at Cape Town harbour to meet her. She got off the boat and promptly broke off the engagement with 'Luke', introduced 'Luke' to Phil and told 'Luke' she was going to marry Phil. It seems she was already married to Phil if you are in possession of the copy of the license. So Phil and Ruth must have met earlier. Phil was a loving man, an actor, poet and painter. 'Luke' never forgave her but he did remain friends with my Father. 'Luke' is dead now. Ruth must have gone to England pregnant. 'Luke' loved her; why did she not tell him? He was a rich man; he would not have shirked his responsibilities. Something else happened. I wish I knew. I hardly know how to answer all the questions? If you are not 'Luke's' son, then I do not know? Do you have any ideas on your father?

By now, my eyes were out on stalks. Some of this was wrong – for example the story about Ma being engaged when she left for England and meeting our Dad on the boat was not about my parents at all, but had happened to some other relatives, long ago. And my jaw dropped at Diane's speculations about this man's possible father. Goodness me!

I began to read his long reply.

From: Mart Bradley
To: Diane
Sent: 3 October, 2011
Subject: RE: Family

Dear Diane
Sorry about the delay in replying, we were out 'till very late last night and I've been waylaid most of the day with a very good friend – hospital visit etc. I did try to write a reply late last night but, given the nature of the task and the fact that I was feeling very emotional, failed somewhat miserably.
Thank you so much for your wonderful reply. I have read

and reread it so many times I feel I almost know the details by heart. I started on this research many years ago with just a name and a story. To finally make contact with my real family and to get such a welcoming, positive response is beyond my wildest dreams. I will attempt to outline everything for you now. Having had a night to think it all over once again, it may be an easier task for me today.

I knew I was adopted from the age of about twelve. My adoptive parents, the Bradleys, were very loving and my childhood is full of great memories. They christened me Martyn Richard. They gave me a loving environment and a good education. I went through grammar school and Higher Education and qualified as a teacher.

A teacher! My goodness, I was a teacher too.

I read on, about how he had learnt he was adopted because of not getting a gold watch one Christmas when he was twelve. I read how he had been born at a home in England called The Haven, and about how he had always believed that he was the result of troubles experienced by a missionary family in the Congo. I kept shaking my head and thinking, 'my goodness!' He went on to tell Diane about his search for his mother, and how it had taken fifty years. He described how the Nelson Mandela Foundation had sent him a photo of the man he believed was his mother's father.

Then followed some details about his life – he had been happily married for a long time, with one daughter, who was 'an army officer, a Captain with the 1st Royal Gurkha Rifles' – I realised this must be some part of the British Army. As I read this, the thought popped up in the back of my mind that, of my mother's three brothers, the two who had survived the war – Frank and Ralph – had both had long careers in the military.

With this man's daughter also in the army, it seemed that the families had much in common.

My eyes were like saucers as I read the next bit:

'It does sound as if "Luke" could have been my father. The timing certainly fits and Ruth may have suspected she was pregnant when she boarded the boat to England. I was not premature, in fact I was a very big baby and went the full 9 months. I don't know the date of her return to South Africa – do you have this? She certainly married Philip between April and June 1951.'

And then I read:

'The thought that I now have a real family still hasn't sunk in yet. You mention Ruth's two daughters. How do you think they will respond to a new brother appearing after all this time? Were they aware of the birth I wonder or was it all kept secret?

The thought of two real sisters is wonderful but the last thing I would want to do is to upset anyone, especially with such an old skeleton in the cupboard!'

Oh my. His letter ended like this:

'Thank you, once again, Diane, for your response to this. I'm so pleased to be welcomed, very emotional at present, and trying to come to terms with the result of 50 years' uncertainty. I have attached all I can think of that's relevant – certificates, The Haven pictures and history, recent family photos, etc.'

I had to admit it – this man sounded quite sane, really nice in fact. My heart began to beat faster, because I realised that all this astonishing stuff was beginning to sound pretty convincing to me, too.

Then I began opening the attachments. There was an adoption certificate, on which I saw that his birth name was given as 'Ralph Allan Wellington'. I saw that my mother's maiden name was indeed there. I saw that his adoptive parents had given him the name 'Martyn Richard Bradley'.

One of the attachments was an article about The Haven, with a picture of the 'Home for Mothers and Babies', the beautiful old mansion where he was born. I scanned through it briefly, deciding to read it properly later.

There was a small certificate from The Haven with Ralph's baby details on it. It gave his birth weight and some instructions about how to feed him. Then there was a Union Castle Line passenger list showing my mother's name and country of origin, as well as a list of UK marriages between April and June 1951, with her name on it. Fevvy and I knew that she and my Dad had married in England before coming to live in South Africa. I began to realise how much research this Ralph-person had done.

But some of the attachments were photographs. I opened the first one. A large clear photo of three people filled the computer screen. A man of about my age, his daughter, and his wife. The man had a moustache and a mop of curly brown hair.

The photo quite took my breath away. I felt as if I'd had an electric shock. I leapt up from the chair, then sat down again, staring with my mouth hanging open. I couldn't believe what I was seeing. This photo was enough. It might be impossible, it could never have happened, but it had. It was true.

There could be no doubt at all. He, this Ralph Wellington/Martyn Bradley person, looked like a rough, male, moustached version of me. And his daughter, Abigail, standing there smiling in the photo, looked a bit like I'd looked when I was young, with the same long brown hair. Even more startling was how much she looked like all of our daughters – my Shirley and Heather, and Fevvy's Laura. She looked more like them, in fact, than they looked like each other. She could be their sister, not their cousin.

There could be no doubt at all. No need for DNA tests or anything like that. No wonder Arthur had chuckled and said he would send me the e-mails.

I grabbed the office phone and dialled Fevvy again. No reply, but I remembered that she had told me she was going out for lunch. So I tried her cellphone number. When she answered, I could hear that she was in a car, but she assured me that her friend Dawn was driving and that we could talk. Actually, this call turned out to be very short. Once I had told her I had seen his photo and that it had convinced me, we both choked up completely.

I was overwhelmed by the enormity of what we were discovering. We had a brother! Where we had always just been two, just Fevvy and me, we were suddenly three. A brother!

There could be no doubt, but I just couldn't believe it. This was the most astonishing and incredible thing that had ever happened to me.

I wandered about the house in a state of shock. Rob would only get in from his work out on the farm at lunchtime. I couldn't phone anyone, as Fevvy was out to lunch and I was not ready to tell anyone else. My thoughts were in total turmoil. I just couldn't believe it. It felt like someone had just died, the level of shock and disbelief was the same, but yet this was actually something wonderful. We had just gained a brother. Unbelievable! I kept returning to the computer to read things, or to look at the photo again. And every time I looked at him, I would exclaim, 'Unbelievable!'

Unbelievable it might be, but what now? What should I do? And then my thoughts turned to Ma. *Ma, what happened?* How I wished that she was still alive. How had she managed to keep something so huge, so devastating, a secret from us? She had kept it a secret her whole life. *Oh Ma!* I felt overwhelmed with sympathy for her. Had Granny, her mom, known about her baby boy? Had anyone known?

Right away I knew what I must do. I would have to dig into the old family letters and albums, and see what I could find out. There just had to be something, some clue somewhere.

Chapter 15
Heather – The phone call

The 4th of October, a Tuesday, started like all other days in Port Elizabeth, perfectly normally. I got up feeling happy and relaxed. It was school holidays and I was at home for a lovely week's break. I still had six more days of peace and quiet ahead of me before facing another hectic term of running the finances of a local school. My friend Dawn was coming to fetch me to go to lunch at a beautiful venue out of town and I was just locking up the house and waiting for Dawn to arrive. The phone rang – nothing unusual about that – and I stopped closing windows and went to answer it. I was delighted to hear my sister's voice – although she did sound a little odd, not quite her normal, enthusiastic self.

'I think you had better sit down, Fev,' she said in a concerned older sister voice after we'd said hello and told each other how we were. Fee and I are very close, we always have been, and kept in contact nearly every day. I said I was quite fine and continued with my tasks. 'Well,' she said rather slowly, 'Arthur has just phoned.'

'Oh, is he coming to visit us all?' I asked. Arthur coming to visit was quite normal and something to look forward to. There was silence for a brief few seconds before Fee continued. 'Well no, Fev,' she said. I was baffled as to why she sounded so concerned and almost puzzled by it all and began to worry whether Arthur had phoned with very bad news – maybe someone in the family had died but I could think of no death that would cause such a reaction. I walked towards the back door to close it and lock up.

'Arthur says we have... ,' she paused, sounding very tense and then started again, '... well, someone in England has contacted the family, who thinks he is related to us.' Another silence and then, 'Um... he says his name is Ralph Allan Wellington.'

'Oh goodness,' I gasped. 'Uncle Ralph's son?' Another silence followed and then I heard Fee's voice coming clearly through the phone.

'Well, no, Fev,' she said, speaking very slowly. 'Not Uncle Ralph's son... *Ma's*.'

I froze, my hand still on the backdoor handle – had I heard Fee correctly? *Ma's son! Impossible!* Shock waves pulsed through my body, and a distant word – brother – started to flash on the horizon of my seemingly paralysed brain, very softly and dimly at first, but coming closer and louder all the time until it was right in front of me. I shook my head. What on earth! Not Ma – we would have known. Not Ma! Not our Ma!

I can't remember what we both said after that but scepticism was top of the list of feelings alongside the shock and, oh yes, DNA testing would definitely be required before we would take any of this seriously. He could make no demands on us we reassured ourselves as our minds struggled to process this life-changing news. What could he be like? If he was Ma's son he should be OK, but our thoughts were flying everywhere. We needed to find out more and so Fee, being the more practical of the two of us, said reassuringly, 'Arthur will be e-mailing me all the documents from Diane very soon and I will forward them to you immediately. We can decide what to do after we have looked at everything.' She sounded more her normal self and after a few more words of disbelief and amazement, we both hung up to await further information.

What we had just heard was too incredible to grasp – our mother, our *sensible* mother, having had a child overseas and no one knowing about it. I felt like I was in some sort of weird dream – none of it could be true.

The doorbell rang and I hurried outside to meet Dawn, pretending nothing strange had happened at all. Well, I thought, it just couldn't be true, so pretending nothing had happened was quite easy. Anyway, Fee would sort it all out.

I climbed into Dawn's little grey car and we set off to fetch Carole, who lived in another suburb of Port Elizabeth. I looked at the houses along the roadside as we passed by and my earlier conversation with Fee began to feel more and more like the dream I was pretending it to be. Not real at all, I smiled to myself. I relaxed into my seat and chatted happily away. Everything was getting back to normal. We rounded the top of a hill and looked down towards the sea and over our beautiful Algoa Bay. Yes, everything was going to be fine.

We stopped a while at Carole's house and discussed some theatre props she and Dawn would be needing for a production they were both involved in, and then all piled into Dawn's little car to head off for lunch in the countryside outside Port Elizabeth. Dawn had just set off when my phone rang again. I saw that the caller was Fee and my heart gave a nervous thump.

'I've received the e-mails,' she managed to say in a tight voice. There was a short silence. 'I've seen his photo.'

I gasped. 'What does he look like?'

There was another silence and then Fee said in a strangled little voice, '*Just like us!*' I heard a muffled sob, and after that we couldn't say anything more to each other.

I alarmed Dawn and Carole as the most incredible wave of emotion washed over me and tears poured down my cheeks. Dawn pulled the car over and stopped abruptly.

'Bag!' (We all call each other 'Bag'.) 'Bag, what's wrong, has someone died?' she asked, patting my knee with concern.

What could I say? How could I possibly explain it to her? Dawn had known our family since I was about thirteen and had been particularly close to Ma.

'No, no,' I managed to bleat between sobs, shaking my head and digging in my handbag for a tissue. 'Fee and I... well...' I swallowed and blew my nose. 'We have a brother. Ma had a son!'

'*Whaaaaat*,' Dawn almost shouted. 'You have a brother?'

'Well, apparently we do,' I said, choking back my tears and starting to calm down a bit. I looked across at her and had to stop myself from bursting into hysterical laughter. She looked so amazed and shocked – just like I felt.

I tried to explain to them the little we knew – Ma being overseas at the time of his birth and giving him up for adoption. But mostly all I was capable of doing was shaking my head and saying, 'Good Lord'. Dawn eventually started driving again and soon we were once more on our way. Trees and bushes flashed past my window but I could take nothing in and didn't appreciate any of the scenery for the rest of the drive out to lunch. It had always been just Fee and me but now we were suddenly *three*. Far too much for my little brain to handle so quickly.

'Bring my friend some wine, quickly,' Dawn instructed the waitress, patting the table in front of me. 'She has just had an enormous shock.'

Oh goodness, but Dawn was making me want to laugh hysterically and I did giggle a bit as I felt totally clueless as to how to cope with the situation. I felt a little better after a few gulps of wine, but my mind just wouldn't function properly.

I have no idea what we ate or what we said. I felt I was in a trance. I could hear Dawn and Carole talking away but could not process what they were saying. 'Good Lord,' I just kept muttering over and over and shaking my head and the two of them were finding it most amusing and of course, quite fascinating as I rambled on and on in my disbelief.

I needed to get home. I needed to see the e-mails but most of all I needed to see the photo.

Eventually the meal was over and we were back in the car and driving home. As we bounced along the narrow winding road and got closer and closer to home – and the computer – I began to feel my tummy starting to knot up. It was quite alarming to realise that yes, I was afraid of what I would read. I was even more afraid of what I would see. Dawn must have realised why I was becoming quieter and quieter and I was very relieved when she said she would stay with me and we could look at the e-mails together. (She confessed to me later that wild horses couldn't have dragged her from my side as she wouldn't have missed the next bit of the fascinating story for anything!) We dropped Carole off and drove the few last kilometres home in nervous silence.

Safely back in the study at home, we sat side by side in front of the computer and waited whilst the incoming e-mails downloaded. This mundane task seemed to take forever.

Finally everything was in and we were able to open Fee's e-mail. 'Here it all is, Fev,' she had written. I clicked on the attachments and scrolled down, not bothering to read anything yet. I held my breath and stopped scrolling when we saw the top of a photograph begin to appear at the bottom of the screen.

'Be brave, Bag,' Dawn encouraged me with a nudge. I took a deep breath and slowly continued to bring the photograph up onto the screen.

Well, just torrents of tears started pouring down my face again and I could say nothing. Ralph was *just like us...* just so like *Ma*! It was unbelievable. He was totally Wellington through and through. Blow all the other documented proof. It was not necessary, the photograph confirmed it all. There was no doubt – we had a brother. He was definitely *one of us*. Next to him in the photo stood a young girl, his daughter Abigail. I looked at her and shook my head in disbelief. If my daughter and Fee's two were all put in a paper bag together and shaken up, out would pop Abi. It was just so incredible. Helen, Ralph's wife stood on the other side of Abi and looked warm and friendly and definitely like someone we would have no trouble loving to bits. Oh goodness, it was just so hard to take in. But it was all there staring me in the face.

Sitting quietly beside me, Dawn was also shaking her head in disbelief. We looked at his birth certificate which showed his mother's name as my mother's maiden name – Dorothy Ruth Wellington. We read his long letter to cousin Diane telling of his birth and adoption and about his fifty-year search for his family.

We read and looked, shook our heads and just sat in front of the computer for nearly an hour. What to do next? I had no idea, but I needed to tell my daughter. I knew she would find it incredible and I just had to speak to her, but I didn't want to tell her anything on the phone. I should have waited a little longer because Laura, knowing me so well, immediately picked up the tension in my voice.

'Nothing's wrong, love, there's just something I want to tell you,' I said rather lamely to her. I couldn't say, 'There's something mind shattering that I need to tell you,' but that's what I really wanted to say. She was still most alarmed and said she would leave work early and come straight over.

I printed the e-mails and a lovely big colour copy of the photograph and spread them all out on the coffee table in the lounge. Dawn bustled off to the kitchen to make some reviving coffee and we sat down on the big comfortable couches and sipped our lovely hot drinks and shook our heads. I tried to sort my thoughts out. How does one tell such a story? Adrian, my lovely husband of just three years, would be home soon. I didn't have to contact my son just yet, as he was working in Cape Town and as I had already phoned Laura, things were being taken care of. What was wonderful and seemed to have been planned by the hand of providence was the fact that Fee had arranged some time ago to visit the very next morning, so we would be together for a couple of days and could sort everything out with each other's help.

In what seemed no time at all, Laura came hurrying up the front stairs, her lovely long blonde hair flying out behind her. Goodness, but she looked like the picture of Abi. She let herself into the hall with her key and walked briskly through to the lounge, her face creased with worry. She stopped abruptly and looked down at the coffee table, her eyes glued to the photograph. 'Who's this?' she said, pointing down at Ralph.

What could I do but smile and say as gently as possible, 'Well apparently, he's my brother,' – gulp – 'he's our brother, Fee's and mine,' I continued. 'Our Ma's son.'

'Whaaat,' said Laura, looking totally aghast and collapsing on the couch behind her. 'Bring me a drink!'

At this we burst out laughing and I began to try to explain it all to her, but everything wanted to come out in a rush. Eventually I had told her all I could and she sat holding the picture and just shaking her head.

'He looks so much like Granny,' she said. 'He looks so much like you and Aunty Fee, and Abi looks like all of us cousins.' She was as stunned as I knew she would be and I could also see that she was loving the excitement of the moment.

It began to slowly dawn on me as well, just how exciting this all was. Actually the most exciting, unbelievable and unexpected thing that had ever happened to us in our lives.

Chapter 16
Fiona – Ma's diary

I t must have been about midnight, and I was tired of tossing and turning. Next to me, Rob was sound asleep, tired after a long day on the farm. I'd been relieved when he had come home for lunch and I could at last tell him the morning's incredible news. He had absorbed it calmly, but with great interest. He had shaken his head at the amazing family likeness in the photos, and agreed with me that this Ralph-person sounded really nice in his e-mail.

I'd had a day like no other; no wonder I couldn't sleep. Even when I had managed to doze a little, my mind had been a whirlpool of thoughts. In the pitch darkness of the Karoo night, I got up quietly and tip-toed out of the room.

Once I reached what used to be my son's bedroom across the passage, I closed the door and turned on the light. Since Doug grew up and left home, his room had unofficially become my study, where I kept all my teaching things. Now, on what used to be Doug's bed lay an old blue suitcase, packed ready for my departure for Port Elizabeth early the next morning. I had filled it with everything I could find that might tell us more about our Ma and that might help us believe the unbelievable – that when she was young she had in fact had a baby and given it up for adoption in England.

In it were several old photo albums that had belonged to my parents. There was a file of family-tree data I had collected over the years. There was an old brown leather satchel with 'A.A. Wellington' embossed in neat old-fashioned capitals across one side of it. This used to be my grandfather's satchel, the grandfather I never knew, the 'missionary' who came out from Cornwall to work in South Africa and who ended up running the Healdtown mission station for seventeen years – the first seventeen years of Ma's life – up until 1944, when he died.

Ma had told us that her father had always kept his sermons in the satchel. In it she had kept all the old family letters and documents in her possession. Since I could remember, it had lain in the bottom drawer of Ma's big old dressing table, and after she had died in 2003, I had taken it home and kept it safe.

Now I took the satchel out of the suitcase and opened it again. During that most astonishing day I had spent hours going through everything in it, looking for clues. Had Ma not left something behind, some evidence of the momentous thing that had happened to her in 1949? So far I had found nothing at all. No letter to Granny explaining things. Nothing.

I had found newspaper clippings that Ma and Granny had carefully kept – old yellowed cuttings containing wedding reports, obituaries, descriptions of funerals, birth and death notices. Uncles, aunts, cousins, distant relatives from Granny's past. There were several newspaper articles about our grandfather when he was still alive, as well as reports on his funeral at Healdtown. There was even the actual hymn sheet and order of service used. I had glanced through everything, and put it all aside, next to me, until the bed was covered in papers.

I'd found small packets of old black-and-white photos, mostly of people unknown to me. There were many letters, some in envelopes and some not. I'd found a whole sheaf of letters written to Granny by many different people on our grandfather's death in 1944. Wonderful letters. A bundle of letters written by Ma to Granny in 1960, detailing events at home – my sister and I were little then. A letter of condolence to my mom, written by my grandfather's sister, Aunt Maggie, on the occasion of Granny's death in 1971.

Then there were two long letters written by Granny to Ma, in England, in early 1950. These two letters I had read before, long ago, at Ma's urging. Ma had told me that Granny had written them in answer to Ma's questions about certain family matters. That afternoon I had taken them out of their envelope and re-read them carefully. In the startling light of suddenly having a brother I had seen things in those two letters, written quite soon after his birth, that convinced me that Granny knew nothing of Ma's secret.

Though I'd found no direct evidence of our brother's birth, yet there was indirect evidence. The first place I'd found a clue had been in Ma's old photo albums. Carefully kept in the corner of our bookshelf were five black books. Ma had often shown them to us when she was still alive, and we had looked at them, but not very intently.

They were all much the same, dating from the 1940s and 50s, with old black leather covers. Their pages were made of dark paper onto which black-and-white photographs had been stuck using photo corners. Three of the albums were small, and two were larger. One of the big ones contained my father's photos of his family and of the war – hundreds of tiny prints all meticulously arranged in rows. The other large one began with my parents' wedding in Oxford in 1951, and continued with a few photos of their honeymoon near Blenheim and pictures of their first home in London.

The small albums were the ones that would be of interest to

me now, as they had belonged to Ma before she was married. One began in 1950, with some lovely photos of Ma at Windsor castle, as well as those from a trip that Ma and a friend had made from England to the Continent. Another contained photos from 1944 to 1948. Photos from Ma's teenage years. Nothing there seemed significant.

The one that had interested me most that afternoon began in January 1949. Neatly titled '22nd January–11th February 1949' were photos of Ma's voyage to England. There was Ma, young and happy-looking, on board ship. Of course, what made me stare at those photos and look very closely at them was realising that she must already have been pregnant, though only just. My goodness. With her baby born in early October, her pregnancy must have started in early January, well before the date of her departure. Later, there were photos of Ma in England, going to the seaside at Bournemouth with friends, and visiting Ireland by boat. All the pages were neatly labelled and dated in Ma's handwriting.

There were photos dated 'May 1949' of Ma in Ireland. Ma looked perfectly slim, though she must already have been four months pregnant. Then, without missing a page, the next batch of photos were labelled 'Christmas in London'. Ma was overseas, a visitor in a new country, seeing everything for the first time, and she had found nothing to photograph in all those months? No, this gap must be deliberate. Here was evidence, though indirect, that something that could not be photographed had happened to Ma between May and the end of that year.

There was a similar and even more convincing gap in Ma's old London diary. That afternoon I had discovered that she had written in it every day until 1st August 1949, and then, suddenly and without skipping a page, the next date in it was 25th November. I'd phoned Fevvy immediately, and after another rather emotional discussion we'd agreed that the gaps in the album and in the diary were evidence, though still indirect, that the crazy, unbelievable thing we had been told that morning could really have happened to our mother.

And now it was the middle of the night and it was because of that old diary that I was wide awake.

Ma had always kept the diary in her father's old satchel, and it had still been there when I had taken the satchel out of the cupboard that afternoon. Now I held the old book in my hands again. Ma had shown it to us when we were young, and we'd read bits of it, but it had seemed to hold nothing of particular interest to us.

It was a large soft-covered brown book, well worn, with the words CROXLEY PEN CARBON BOOK printed on its front. Across the top of the cover was printed:

'FROM .... TO........................... No......'

and Ma had filled it in to read *From South Africa to England, No.2*, with a subtitle, *England*.

I opened the book and read, in Ma's handwriting, across the top of the first page: '*Here beginneth the second reading...*' So this was the second volume of her diary. I wondered if the first still existed somewhere, perhaps hiding in the drawer where I kept other things that had belonged to my parents. I would look. The writing was blue and slightly fuzzy, indicating, as I already knew, that these were carbon copies of letters that Ma had written to her mother back home in South Africa.

Taking a blanket through to the lounge, I put it and the diary down next to the couch and went to the kitchen to make myself a cup of tea.

At last, I propped myself up comfortably with cushions, and began to read.

Friday 20th May, 1949

During lunch hour today Mrs Madge took me to what was known before the war as the 'danger zone' – where all the large textile firms stored their goods – all inflammable. It's now a flat area of rubble – Jerry saw to that!! Had a look at St Bartholomew's church – one of the oldest in London – must get inside sometime soon. Plenty of work kept me busy today – I'm beginning to get the hang of it too and feel almost at home with the thereins, therefores, therefor (note subtle difference) etc.

It's raining now but the forecast promises a fine sunny weekend.

It sounded like Ma had just started a new job. I realised that this must have been after the trip to Ireland documented in the photo album. I remembered her telling us that she had gone to England to study at a secretarial college, but they had found that she already knew all they could teach her, so they'd given her a certificate and turned her out. Her first job was for a legal firm, near the Old Bailey. So this was it.

As I read on through the descriptions of her life in London, I remembered that this was why we had struggled to read her diary before – nothing much happened. But now I was determined to read it all. The great surprise of the day made me feel that every word was now important.

Here is an entry that appeared perfectly innocent, but now might mean a lot:

Wednesday 25th May

During lunch hour today I visited St Thomas' hospital and had a blood test – necessary before the U.Castle Line will accept my return passage booking. Incidently they sent me a notice saying there was a cabin for me on the 'Capetown Castle' sailing 1st December and would I send them 73 pounds if I wanted it. I don't – am returning next Oct. or November.

Worked like a galley slave today again. Really enjoy it.

So Ma had visited the hospital for a blood test. Surely they would have found out that she was pregnant? Fascinated, I sipped my tea as I read on.

Thursday 26th May

Had a thoroughly busy day today but loved it as usual. Funny what a kick I get when I finally sit down and put 25 signed letters into their envelopes and send them off. Ann – one of the senior girls – asked me to dinner as she is going on leave – so we went to the Rising Sun, a pub on the corner, and had the most marvellous beef steak and kidney pie I have tasted since I left home. Really well made and real meat, too – new potatoes and peas. Nice pud. Cheese and biscuits and coffee.

I have my morning coffee at the Bailey Mew – the pub next door – they have equally good coffee and tea cakes that are still hot with lovely butter.

Found out from the U. C. Line that they made a mistake about the blood test – thought I was immigrating to S.A. Still, the visit to St Thomas' hospital was worthwhile and most interesting.

The diary went on and on, just like that, with no more visits to the hospital mentioned. I found her handwriting difficult to decipher, especially since the carbon paper had rendered everything a rather blurry blue. But there on the couch in the dark and quiet of the middle of the night I kept on reading, being drawn into the life of the young girl in London, the girl who became my mother, the mother I thought I knew and whose life I thought I had understood.

There was an entry for every day, Ma telling her mother something about her life in London. She must have torn the top copies out of the pen carbon book and mailed them in batches, with perhaps a page of greetings attached.

Friday 17th June

How quickly one accepts things – I wish I could remember what picture I had of the London Underground tubes before I left home – I can well remember my first trip which was from here to Leicester Square. I remember nearly dying of fright and thrill when we got there and I saw a fast moving escalator that I had to get on. I held my breath and then stepped quickly on to the centre of the bottom stair. It's the deepest one in London, being equivalent to nearly 3 stories. Now I just dash with the crowd and run onto the thing which is flat for about 2 yards so that have plenty of time to get onto a step. I used to cling madly to my ticket and hand it carefully to the bloke at the top – for inspection if I was merely changing to another line – now I hold it between my fingers as I pass him just to show I have it and walk past as if I own the whole system. I used to wonder how these hundreds and thousands of folk could look so completely at ease and disinterested but now I stand and can easily pick out the newcomers to London – they look so bewildered and lost and yet so thrilled.

Work went with the usual swing and laugh – I've just been for a walk on the Heath and am now going to bed with the sun – it being about 9.30. It's light until 11pm and then light again (enough to read by) by 4am.

The next day's entry had me sitting up straight, my eyes wide:

Saturday 18th June

I had made arrangements to go down to see someone in Yateley today and certainly couldn't have chosen a more perfect day. Left straight after breakfast, caught a tube to Waterloo, the Southern Line train to Camberley, a bus to Yateley and a taxi to my final destination about a mile out in the country.

The country looks a dream of colour and green trees. Got back fairly early – am going to listen to my Saturday night theatre while I do some sewing.

Here was something at last! This was worth staying up all night for. Yateley was a name I had never heard of until today, but was now seared into my mind. A mile out of Yateley, in the country along Vigo Lane, was The Haven.

Chapter 17
Fiona – The Russells

Having found that reference to Yateley, I was further from sleep than ever. With a second cup of tea in hand I settled myself on the couch, wiped my eyes, and picked up Ma's diary again.

Sunday 19th June

Had a lot I wanted to do today – washing, ironing, sewing and so on. Gosh in this country I don't know how people get any free time – but it's a good place and I get along with my washing and ironing very well now.

Monday 20th June

Had a lovely surprise today at work which opened with the usual thick wad of letters and then Mr Norman called me and sat me down in his office. He said he understood Pam would be back either on Wednesday or next week but would I stay on as long as I could – I had told him I was going away sometime in July and I only have permission from the Ministry of Labour to do full temp work until the end of July. Then Mr Norman said if I'd like a full-time job with the firm when I come back for the winter would I ring them or call, when he would be pleased to take me on their permanent staff. Was it nice to listen to! I said I had been lucky –

and he said it cut both ways. Good old Norman – I think I might well go back there – I like the work, people and City of London very much but can't decide whether I want to work with wills and dead bods all the time – divorce cases etc. Still have loads of time in which to decide.

Much later I realised that on this day Ma's boss was offering her permanent employment – a wonderful compliment to her competence. But all I noticed in the middle of the night was Ma mentioning that she planned to go away 'sometime in July', and it seemed like she would only get back to London 'for the winter'. After the baby, I realised. Now that she had been to Yateley, her arrangements must already have been made. Wow. I shook my head. This still felt totally unbelievable.

I read on. Ma described in detail for her mom a play she went to, as well as a concert. The June entries continued with little of significance – until the end of the month:

Wednesday 29th

Thursday 30th

Both yesterday and today I've had 2 full day's work at the office doing tomorrow's work too. I piled in there today and got some very pretty farewell speeches. Very nice too.

Here she was getting farewell speeches – it seemed she was working until the end of June, and no further. I wondered what she would do, now that she had stopped work. Her baby was due in only three months' time.

Next, I was amused at Ma's comments on the London heat:

Monday 4th July

It's been a really blazing hot day – the hottest in years, but it's glorious – not really any more muggy than P.E. or any coastal town in summer and far pleasanter as there is no wind. People who say they have been hotter in London than in S.Africa delude themselves. They imagine they should always feel cool and cold over here so when it's too hot for a jersey 'it is scorching'. The

English are not used to it and look washed out and like lappies [rags], but it's absolute nonsense as I've proved in the last 3 weeks, and I am one who loathes the summer generally.

These comments about the heat reminded me of something that Ma had once told us about escaping the London heat and going to the country for six months. I was sure I had seen something in the satchel about that. I told myself that tomorrow, once I got to Fevvy's house, I must look through the documents again and see if I could find what Ma had written. For the very next diary entry was about her leaving London and going off to the country. She must have told her mother about it briefly in a covering letter, but the diary just told the story like this:

Tuesday 5^{*th*} *July*

London–Surrey

Was lucky with taxis and porters and made the 9.54 from Waterloo with nearly 20 minutes to spare and got down here just after 11 – on the station a very pleasant faced man – greying hair, rather frail looking and as I imagine James Hilton's Mr Chipps looked at the same age – he turned out to be there to meet me – and was of course Dr. Russell. I heard that he was in the Indian Army until about 1930 when Jennifer was born and he realized that things were going bad and it wouldn't be long before the army cracked up (as it did do) so he cleared out and took up medicine, qualifying in 1938 – did locums etc. during the war – went to Ireland in 1946 to specialize and then bought this practice – a charming man with a very pleasant manner – I just cannot imagine him in the Indian Army.

Back here at his rather delightful home I met Mrs. Russell – a tall well-built, blond woman who looks much too young to have a grown-up daughter – a kind English woman who is generous and hearty but not obvious, then Jennifer – hale and hearty and 19, with more sense than any girl I've met here of her age – keen on sewing, knitting, reading, walking and Danny Kaye!!! Not a bit shy or anything like that about her.

To continue with the introductions there is, in order of importance, Madelein who walks about looking for an opportunity to climb up on a bed or the couch. She has two offspring of 8 months – Delight – who is on heat so confined to a small space under the kitchen table, but remains cheerful and always welcomes any visitors. Her brother Johnathan is everywhere all at once with anybody's shoes, wool, needles – anything – and feels he is easily the most important member of the household. These latter three are bull terriers – white stub-nosed, pink-eyed, animals like old Jock at Wilton. One thing one has to get used to is hearing first hubby, then daughter, then any animal each called 'darling' in quick rotation – it is something that is done in all English homes apparently – from the highest to the lowest.

From my window I look out on the back garden bordered by a mass of trees – the garden is a very large lawn scattered over with odd beautiful rose bushes, lavender, oh and heaps of other flowers.

After unpacking and a late dinner, Jen and I took deckchairs out into the sunny garden and sat knitting, chatting and listening to my personal radio.

Jen, 1950 – Ma's album

On reading further, I discovered that the Russells lived near Camberley, conveniently near Yateley and The Haven, though these places were never mentioned. How I wished that Ma were still alive, that I could ask her about the Russells – how she had made contact with them, and why they had taken her in. She seemed to have been treated like one of the family, taking the dogs for walks with Jennifer, doing needlework, playing cards with the doctor in the evening, helping with household chores, but not having a specific job.

Thursday 7th July

After lunch we put two of the dogs on leads (Delight is still kept locked up) and took them, straining madly on their leads, out onto the common. I was amazed at the huge stretch of it and it's exactly like the country round P.E. Hard stoney ground with loads of heath, heather and such like. Of course masses of oaks every now and then which made it essentially English. There are a couple of huge aerodromes round here and the planes are always zooming over. Especially noticeable are the jets – they make a ghastly noise like a bomb and by the time you look at the 'noise' the plane is nearly out of sight – can they move!

Soon Ma was writing about the heat again, but this time contradicting what she'd said while still in London.

Monday 11th July

Jen started work today – but it was so hot that Mrs R. and I did little but potter around – went shopping this morning at the local stores – took the dogs out on the heath after supper but didn't go far as a fire was raging and the fire engines were on the warpath.

Tuesday 12th July

I take back all I said about the attitude towards the heat – at home our houses are built to keep cool and one manages it more or less – anyway it's not the thick oppressive mugginess that has been here today – we even had a siesta after dinner, not that it helped – it's as hot inside as in the sun – everybody looks half baked and washed out. The weather forecast says it's going to break soon – possibly tomorrow – we all had little sleep last night – I spent the night putting on my light – reading and then putting it out to try and sleep. At about 3 Mrs. Russell came in – said she was too hot to sleep and could smell burning. We discovered it came from outside so retired again, but it was getting light before we all fell asleep. The strikes at the London docks are getting serious. France are thinking of joining in. Communistic element of course. The king has proclaimed a State of Emergency.

Thursday 14th July

Received lovely food parcel packed by Wilton and Dugmore – all sorts of lovely bits and pieces which we shall enjoy. Overcast today but still very close and most oppressive.

I was interested to read about a food parcel, and realised that London in those days was still feeling the aftermath of the war, with rationing still in force. No wonder Ma often wrote about food, especially meat, with such feeling.

I'd been reading so intently that I'd forgotten my tea – I drank it down in one lukewarm gulp and carried on.

Next day, Ma was accompanying the doctor on some of his rounds. She'd been with the Russells for ten days by then. I remembered that her sister Lylie had been a doctor, and that Ma had at one time wanted to be a doctor too. She had told us how she had 'helped Lylie in the clinic at Healdtown', so I supposed Dr. Russell had noticed her interest in medical things.

Friday 15th July

Jennifer and Dr. R. both celebrated their birthdays today so we started off bright and early. I went the rounds with Dr. and drove miles through narrow country lanes lined with thick trees and ferns etc. Met various of his patients, who were all very nice, and then visited a 'hut settlement' – old army places like huge tanks cut in half longways – crowded with people. Horrible conditions to live under but at least it's a roof over the poor types' heads...

How I wished I had taken the trouble to read this diary properly while Ma was still alive. Perhaps she would have told me her secret if I had asked the right questions and been sympathetic enough. A memory suddenly struck me – when I was quite young, possibly still a teenager, the daughter of a close friend of

Ma's had had an illegitimate child. There had been no secret about it, the rather plump girl had simply said nothing and no one had suspected anything until one day she had gone into labour and shocked her family rigid. I remembered how Ma had spoken to us about this – we had later met the little child – and I knew that she had been sympathetic and understanding towards her friend. Sympathetic and unjudgmental. There'd been someone else too who had told Ma that she had secretly given up a child for adoption, whom Ma had listened to without condemnation. Oh my word, now it all made sense.

Saturday 16th July

We all rolled down to breakfast this morning feeling very fit and full of the joys except for doctor, who had had two calls to babies during the remaining few hours of the night.

Sunday 17th

We spent a very lazy Sunday – I have been reading 'Pride and Prejudice' – have seen the play and the film but never read it before – am thoroughly enjoying it – most amusing and entertaining. Started to rain after dinner and everything looks drenched.

Today has been Dr.'s unlucky day – he's been out on call all day and now (10.30 pm) has just dashed off again – two of his babies got stuck and he used instruments and had to work hours on each to keep them alive. I believe he's really good – anyway he saved them both.

Interesting to see how often Dr. Russell seemed to be delivering babies. Then I stopped and stared at that mention of 'Pride and Prejudice'. An image flashed into my mind – a slim red book in Ma's hands – my old school copy of 'Pride and Prejudice'. Ma, sitting in the smaller cottage she had moved to after our Dad had died, holding the book in her hands – she had asked me to bring her a copy of it.

On and on the diary went. I came across an entry where Ma told her mother about her feelings for the Russells:

Monday 25th July

Like all English people I find they 'grow' on one and wear well. Even when you like them right from the start, they seem to get nicer and nicer as they relax and finally take you into their confidence or establish a friendship that one feels will last.

Towards the end of the month, it was Ma's birthday. I noticed that alongside the date in the diary she had added, in a modern red felt-tipped pen: '*1949 (22nd birthday)*'. This was something she must have added to the diary later, quite recently in fact. I realised that there were quite a few marks in that red pen, all over the diary. Page numbers and the like. So this was the day Ma turned twenty-two:

Friday 29th July [1949 (22nd birthday) added in red pen]

Old age creeping on! Mrs R. presented me with a lovely chocolate cake iced with boiled condensed milk and we had quite a tea party.

Dr. drove us to Camberley this afternoon and we spent hours in a dress shop. I fell for a lovely navy and white outfit but luckily had left my cheque book behind, not that it has much to its credit.

I felt sure this must have been written to camouflage the truth, for she would not have fitted into ordinary clothes by then at all, being almost seven months pregnant. I wondered how she was coping with it all; finding maternity clothes to wear and other items she might need for the birth.

Saturday 30th July

We had supper latish and picnic-style last night and then I went out with Dr. to see a little girl who was ill – just for the drive – a perfect night – lovely and cool out – we had to go along a dreadful road through the country – got back 11.30.

And here, the last entry before the gap. Ma and Jen alone at the house, as Dr. and Mrs Russell had gone away for a few days.

Monday 1st August, August Bank Holiday

We shot up early this morning and what an orgy of tidying we had. Did all the laundry, dusted, polished and vacuumed...

Having finished my fairisle jersey am now going up to iron it before sewing it up. Will enclose the pattern with this. I used the exact colours but changed over the green and yellow and am making a plain long-sleeved cardigan in the green to match.

And there, with no warning, the August narrative ended. No explanation given, though Ma's handwriting in those last few sentences seemed a little more spread out than usual, as if she knew this would the last entry for a long time.

Had she then moved to The Haven? She must have.

I read on. With no pages left out or missing, the diary continued – but with a gap in time of nearly four months. I marvelled at it again, and at the way Ma pretended to have lost her diary for all those months:

Friday November 25ᵗʰ [emphasised in red felt-tipped pen]

Northcote House – Blackwater

Having got my diary back, I had better make use of it! I decided that I'd go back to London for the winter and instead of going up on Monday would go today, fix a job etc. and then come back and have a good weekend with the Russells – so up at some ungodly hour and on the 9am train arriving at Waterloo 10.5.

'Northcote House, Blackwater' was a place I had never heard of, but on reading further I realised that it must be the address of the Russells, though Ma never said so. Then followed a long and detailed account of Ma's day in London, having an interview at a hospital for a post as a secretary, and visiting her old office, where she was welcomed with open arms. She then took a train back to the Russells, where again she received a warm welcome – she wrote that she caught *the 4.24 back from Waterloo – got a taxi here and found Jen waiting with practically a red carpet laid on!*

At first I got confused, before I realised that Ma, writing from the Russells' house, was writing in the evening of the day she went to London. The 'red carpet' meant that she had not been back to the Russells until the evening, and was seeing Jen for the first time in a long while. So she must have left for London straight from The Haven. My goodness.

I noticed too that she wrote that she *had decided to go back to London for the winter* – but surely she had already decided that long ago? I looked back in the diary and saw that on 20th June, when Mr Norman had offered her a permanent post, they had spoken of her coming back *for the winter*. Was Ma's cover story slipping? (Only a few days later did we fully understand the reason why she was so rattled that day, the 25th of November.)

The diary went on to describe her weekend with the Russells, and then she returned to London on the Sunday:

Sunday 27th Nov ['1949' added in red pen]

LONDON

I got up early – made tea for Dr. and followed it up by making and taking up breakfast. Jen and I took the dogs out before lunch, which we had round about 2 pm. Dr. and Mrs R. went out to tea and we were entertained by a rosy-cheeked teenager boyfriend of Jen's whom she scorns but who seemed very nice.

I just managed to make the train at Camberley 6.40 and so arrived back here just before 7.50. Mrs C. made me some tea and sandwiches – I've unpacked and am quite ready to fall into bed.

Ma had mentioned 'Mrs C.' before: she was her landlady in London – so now Ma had returned to board with her once again.

It seemed that the significant part of the diary was over, but I kept reading. There followed a really long letter, undated because the first page was missing, describing first an interview at the firm George Cohen and Sons and then going on to document her first few days of work there. She started work on Thursday 1st December, and the letter was completed the following Monday. What interested me was that Jennifer Russell came to visit her that weekend.

She loves London and this is the only way I can repay them and anyway she's a nice kid and we get on really well together. I met her at Waterloo and we went along to Piccadilly for dinner at a rather nice Corner House – orchestra laid on. Piccadilly Circus was brilliantly lit and really looked wonderful.

'This is the only way I can repay them,' – what wonderful people the Russells must have been to have Ma, a complete stranger, come and stay with them like that. She had obviously grown to love them.

She and Jen saw some of the London shops and then went flat-hunting – Jen had an interest in where Ma would stay because it seemed that she too planned to come and work in London and possibly stay with Ma, sometime in the future.

The next and last entry in the diary was the beginning of a letter written from Ma's new flat:

Malvern House Hotel

29 Holland Park Avenue

11th December, 1949

Mum darling,

I was going to write a letter card to you but I know once I start nattering I just don't stop and it would mean 2 cards and that's 1/= so it doesn't save. Yes I'm having a great saving campaign now – a case of needs must – what a country. Everybody is broke! …

For Ma, this was surely the result of not working for all those months. I noticed too that she mentioned 'letter cards'. I wondered what they were – like postcards, maybe? Perhaps this meant that she had written only occasional brief messages to her mother while she was at The Haven, fearing that she wouldn't be able to write long letters there without revealing the truth. I was convinced she had pretended to lose her diary so that she could keep writing to her mother for those four momentous months, without having to describe her daily life. Thus she had been able to conceal the birth of her son. A secret she had kept for the rest of her life.

Chapter 18
Fiona – Travelling

My bakkie knew the way perfectly. It knew when to slow down to walking pace to negotiate the many ruts in the road made by some not-too-recent rains. It knew when a particularly stony place in the dusty surface was coming, and would crawl carefully over it. It could anticipate all the really sharp turns as the road wound its way through the hills west of Jansenville. My bakkie seemed to negotiate everything sensibly by itself, without any effort on my part, for I was in another world. Even the veld, a smattering of short twisted trees on a moth-eaten carpet of low Karoo bushes and dried grasses, passed by without my noticing it. Usually I loved to look at everything, enjoying the open sparsely-covered plains, the thickly bushed ravines and the spekboom-covered hillsides on the way, taking note when the veld was green, after rain, or grey and brown where it was dry. That day I noticed nothing.

My world was Ma's world, a young girl in London in 1949, secretly pregnant and having to make arrangements to have her baby, cheerfully writing diary-letters home while all the time dealing with this huge crisis. Ma's London whirled in my mind as my bakkie wound its way along the rough Karoo road.

I could see her typing letters at the legal firm near the Old Bailey, and going to a nearby pub for lunch, where they somehow managed to provide real butter in that time of post-war rationing. I could see her catching a tube home to Mrs C.'s, and doing her laundry and ironing in the evenings. I could see her visiting the great old London churches, and going to the flicks with friends. What I still found incredibly hard to believe was what was going on behind it all, the hidden story that she so skilfully concealed behind those friendly letters to her mother.

I thought about the other old letters I had read the day before, and especially the one that had convinced me that, even after the event, Granny had known nothing of Ma's secret. The phrases that had startled me were etched into my brain and I mulled over them as I drove.

When Ma was about twelve, her sister Lylie, a newly-qualified doctor, suffered from severe depression. Doctors could do nothing for her, and eventually, tragically, she committed suicide. Ma had told us that ten years later, when she was in England, she had written to her mother asking her to explain things to her that she had been too young to understand. Ma had kept Granny's long and detailed reply, and had shown the letter to us while she was still alive. Yesterday, I'd found it in my grandfather's satchel and read it again.

It was dated 19th April 1950. AFTER Ralph's birth, I now realised. I read it all carefully, looking for anything that would tell me if Granny had known Ma's secret.

In those days, depression wasn't generally recognised as an illness. Granny wrote that people tried to give Lylie advice, suggesting that if she confessed her *secret sins* she would feel better. Granny described how they said that if Lylie would *share and reveal what it was which was causing this distress of mind etc. she would be cured.* Granny concluded, *Poor Lylie tried to think of the sins she had committed and though as she said to me, she had*

had thoughts of which she was not proud, she could not think that she was being punished like this for them. M [an aunt] said to her if she had a baby hidden somewhere to confess it and she at least would not condemn. It's ludicrous if it were not so tragic, don't you think.

My goodness me, imagine Ma reading this in April 1950. I was sure that Granny, whom I had known as a lovely gentle and kind person, could not have written like this if she had known that, just a few months before, Ma had had the agony of giving away her little baby boy for adoption.

No, besides the evidence of the diary, where Ma had so carefully not revealed anything, I was sure that Granny had never known.

The more I thought about it, the more I was convinced that our Dad couldn't have known Ma's secret, either. He had been a wonderful, innocent, idealistic person, largely unaware of many of the unhappier things in life. Supremely romantic too, the most lovable man, he had idealised my mother and thought the world of her. I felt sure that when Ma first met him in London in late 1950, she had found she couldn't tell him of her illegitimate son.

Secondly, there was something our Dad had once said, that now, in my present state of shock, came to my mind with a jolt. I could remember climbing the mulberry tree in our garden after hearing it, so it must have happened when I was still quite young, perhaps just into my teens. A couple who lived nearby were getting divorced, and my parents had been discussing this sad development. At one point my Dad had said that it was good that they had not yet had children, for, in his opinion, once a couple had a child they were married forever in God's eyes. I had not noticed my mom's reaction to this, probably she'd just shrugged and let it pass, and I had later climbed our huge old mulberry tree and thought about divorce in general, not about Ma at all. But now I saw the significance of what my Dad had said. He could never have spoken like that had he known about Ma's first child.

All too soon I came up over a rise in the road and could see the little town of Jansenville in the distance, spread out over some low hills. As I drove into the sleeping town, I felt relieved to see that there was no car waiting at our agreed meeting place. My violin pupil had not yet arrived. I did a u-turn and then parked in the wide empty street that passes right through the little town on its way from Graaff-Reinet to Port Elizabeth. I sat and waited. Behind me, fast asleep on the back seat of my bakkie, were two teenage girls whom I had fetched from a farm near ours and who would also be playing in the youth orchestra.

The road was lined with a few shops and single-storied houses, most with verandahs right around them or at least in front; typical houses built to withstand the African heat.

At this early hour, there was no traffic at all. I sat watching my rearview mirror, and within a minute or two saw a small white car coming down the hill towards me. It must be them. Sure enough, they drew up behind me and I found myself greeting my friend and her son, David, as if nothing out of the ordinary had just happened to me. I was proud of David, a wonderfully talented pupil of mine who would be playing his violin near the front of the orchestra. I introduced him and his mom to the sleepy girls, who revived impressively at the sight of a sweet, good-looking teenage boy, and we chatted for a moment, mostly just lamenting the earliness of the hour, before setting off again in opposite directions. The road was easy now, wide, tarred and mostly straight, and I had it almost all to myself.

I remember chatting briefly to David, who sat in the seat next to me, expressing my hope that he would enjoy his time in the orchestra. This was something that happened most years – one or two of my pupils would be sufficiently advanced to audition for the orchestra workshop, which took place during the October school holidays, and would travel there with me. We would stay at Fevvy's house, and I would take them to the venue every day and sit in on each session myself, loving seeing how the conductor could take this large group of young musicians – who mostly had never played together before and sounded quite scratchy at first – and mould them into something that made the most beautiful music. It was wonderful.

But this time I knew things would be different. Even as we set off I was glad that David was generally a quiet chap and wouldn't want to talk too much. So early in the morning – especially for teenagers – it wasn't long before he lapsed into silence. The two girls were completely quiet, and must have been asleep. At once my bakkie engaged auto-pilot and I was off again, my head whirling with the shocks, puzzles and discoveries of the day before.

The previous afternoon, in going through the contents of my grandfather's satchel, I had found my Granny's little address book. It was a slim pocket book, and hand-written on its pale red leather cover was the word 'Keep' – I was so glad Ma had done that. I couldn't wait to reveal the little book to Fevvy, and to show her what I had found in it.

It was filled with addresses written in Granny's unique handwriting. At the back was a long list of family birthdays, with the names of all Granny's children and grandchildren, including Ma's and Dad's, and Fevvy's and mine. But not Ralph's.

I found a small photo of Ma when young, stuck into the book on a page with a London address. How beautiful she looked. Soon I recognised this as a copy of Ma's passport photo, for I found her passport in the satchel too. It had been issued in 1948.

Ma had always told us that she went to England to study at a secretarial college. It had sounded to us as if the trip had been planned well in advance, and was not a hurried escape. This was borne out by something else that I found in the little address book:

a letterhead from a secretarial college in London, cut off a letter and pasted into the little book. Now this I had found fascinating, for the letterhead was dated 18th November 1948. It confirmed to me again that Ma had made arrangements to go overseas well before she fell pregnant.

Later in the book, still in the 'Wellington' section, I had found another letterhead that Granny had carefully pasted in, this time of the George Cohen Company – the firm where Ma worked when she returned to London after having her baby.

It looked like Ma had had several London addresses, and they were all recorded there in Granny's handwriting, but of those four months when Ma must have stayed at The Haven, there was no trace.

I had scanned right through the little book, looking for any indication that Granny knew about Ma's baby, and I had found none. No reference to The Haven, no address in Yateley, nothing at all, anywhere.

So if Ma had kept it a secret from her mother, and later also our father, was there anyone back home who had known about her baby? I doubted it. We would have to ask Ma's closest friends. Aunty Moira was still alive and living in PE – she had been at school with Ma, and it was she whose daughter had surprised her family by suddenly having a baby. I wondered if Ma had perhaps confided in her. (Later Fevvy and I visited her, and she listened to our story with ever-widening eyes and with growing understanding of her life-long friend. No, Ma had not told her her secret, she said, but now at last she understood why Ma had been so kind to her at the time of her daughter's shock addition to the family.)

Another close friend of Ma's was her brother Ralph's wife, Gwen, whom we had called Aunty Fluffy. She had been a wonderfully sympathetic, understanding woman – it was a pity that she was no longer alive. Perhaps Ma had entrusted her with her secret?

And then, finally, the big question. What about the baby's father? Who was he? And had he known? Round and round my head it went, behind every other question this was always there, always in my mind. If Ralph's photo hadn't been so convincing, I would still be insisting that for Ma to have had a child before she was married was quite impossible. And as to who the father was, the more I thought about everything, the more I became sure that though Diane had been wrong about some things in her first letter to Ralph, she was most probably right about this one thing. I had felt she was a little premature in airing her speculations so soon, but still, I had to admit to myself, she could be right. Little things that Ma had said at various times in her life kept coming back to me. Nothing had meant much to me on its own, but all added up, they pointed to one thing – that the man from her past called 'Luke' was probably Ralph's father.

If this was so, I was sure that Ma had most definitely never told him her secret. She had left South Africa before she could have been sure of her pregnancy, perhaps before she had even suspected it, and when she returned, she was married to our Dad. Little things she had said to us seemed to indicate that she had resented 'Luke' all her life, and had made sure she never saw him again.

Oh Ma. What a burden to carry. Not only the secret, but more importantly, what it meant. What it meant to her to give up a child and never know what had happened to him. It had certainly affected her deeply – I felt as if I was only now beginning to understand my mother for the first time. One of the most difficult things about her had been her emotional dependence on Fevvy and me, especially after we both got married. She seemed unable to let us go. If we didn't phone her often, like every second or third day, she would be upset. It was as if she was afraid she might lose us.

Again as I drove, I found myself shaking my head. (Next to me, young David was not asleep, but quietly staring out at the long straight tar road ahead. I hoped he didn't think I was shaking my head at him.) How hard it must have been for Ma to endure that loss her entire life, and never be able to talk about it. How hard to keep such a burdensome secret, and to keep it so well. Especially for someone like herself, who liked to talk openly. My goodness. She must have ached to tell someone.

I realised that when I got to PE, I must phone Ma's old minister and find out if she had ever confided in him. He was a wonderful man who had known my parents for more than thirty years and had conducted both of their funerals. Surely Ma would have trusted him enough to tell him, especially in that last year after our Dad died?

The road went on and on, the 2½ hour journey giving me plenty of time to think. My mind was full of Ma and what she had gone through, but I had sympathy for what adoptive parents went through too. Rob and I were close to a couple who had adopted a son, and had seen how intensely emotional the whole process was. There was the deep sadness, experienced over many years of disappointment, of not being able to have a child of one's own. Then the anxiety of waiting and hoping and longing to find a baby to adopt – sometimes it took a long time. Then at last the intense joy of finally receiving a child, and even then the agonising worry that he might be taken back by the biological parents before the legal period of waiting was over. And then still, later, having to tell him that he was adopted, and hoping that he would adjust to this information well. The whole process was fraught with pain, but also full of the joy of having a child to love.

So it was pain mixed with joy. Seeing things now from the side of the biological mother, I realised that in Ma's case, the pain of losing her son had never been softened by the joy of meeting him in later life and finding out how he had got on. For her, the loss was total and final.

My head was reeling – reeling, I realised, just like it had when each of our parents had died. Our Dad had died in 2002 at the age of eighty-seven, quietly and peacefully of heart failure after a week in hospital. His death had not been a surprise, and yet in the middle of the night when the sister phoned to tell us 'your father's condition has deteriorated', and we had hurriedly got Ma ready to take her there in her wheelchair, and had arrived in his ward to find that he had already slipped away, even then there was a horrible feeling of shock and unreality, together of course with deep sorrow. In the days following his death we had felt as if we couldn't believe it, that it couldn't be true that we would never see him again.

I had felt like that after Ma's death, too. As my bakkie sailed smoothly along on the good tar road, I thought about it all again. Her death was a little more unexpected than Dad's, even though she had been ill for several years, needing to be permanently on oxygen. It was in July 2003, and Rob and I and the children were away from the farm on holiday. Ma had been delighted when she heard of our plans, and had encouraged us to go.

We were going to Hogsback, a place where she had been happy when she was young. Her father had been governor of the Healdtown Mission Station, where Ma grew up. Ma told us that when she was about five years old (about 1932), he had built a simple wooden holiday house in the mountains nearby, at Hogsback. He had named the house Trewennan, a Cornish name, because he came from Cornwall, Ma had told us. The family spent a lot of time at Hogsback, and Granny even lived there when she left the Mission Station after our grandfather died in 1944.

TREWENNAN and the HOGSBACK

Dad's drawing of the Trewennan house

When I was young we used to go there for holidays, and Fevvy and I had loved the old house. It was only in the late 1960s, after the house had burnt down in a dreadful fire, that the property was sold.

So then, in the winter of 2003, I was going back there for the first time in many years. Ma was weak and ill at the time, suffering from heart failure and breathing problems, but she was happy to think of us going to Hogsback.

She was happy too because we planned to visit Healdtown on our way home. Fevvy and I had never been there. I think this must have been because by the time we were born, Healdtown was quite different from what it had been when Ma was growing up. The new government had taken control of mission schools, taken them away from the church and had brought in the apartheid policy of deliberately withholding a proper education from people of colour. I could still hear Granny's indignant voice saying, 'Wicked! It's wicked!' during a family discussion about that. Now in her old age, Ma was happy about our plans to visit Healdtown, for she had loved it, the place where she spent the first seventeen years of her life. But she warned us that we would find it in ruins.

Of course, we never did get to Healdtown that weekend, for Ma died while we were still at Hogsback. Rob and I and the children had a wonderful few days there, hiking to many of the amazing waterfalls that Ma had told us about, and also visiting the site of the original house her father had built. I phoned her often, asking her many questions. For example, when we visited the new house on the old Trewennan site, I called her to ask her, 'What is the old moss-covered brick structure that is still here in the garden?' and she told me, delightedly, that it was the old bread oven that they had used in the early days. Because it was outside, it had not been destroyed in the fire.

During that same telephone call, I told Ma of our plans to climb Hog 1, the highest peak in the Hogsback. I expressed my worries that we might not manage it, as the mountain looked so high and intimidating. 'Oh you will, you will,' she said happily. I knew that she loved that mountain, and that as she sat in her room talking to me on the phone, she was actually looking at it, for my father's large oil painting of the three Hogs hung on the wall opposite her chair.

We duly climbed the mountain, and were delighted with the amazing views from the top. After a happy family picnic and many photos next to the trig beacon, I dialled Ma's number. I wanted to tell her that she was right, that we had made it to the top as she had said we would, and that we too loved her mountain.

She didn't answer as quickly as she usually did. Her phone rang and rang. When at last someone picked up, instead of hearing Ma's voice, I heard the sister in charge of the retirement village. Very flustered, she told me that my mother was seriously ill, had 'completely collapsed'. I immediately phoned Fevvy. She answered rather groggily, as she was ill in bed with flu, but said she would get into her car and go to Ma right away.

By then Rob and the children were ready to start their descent of the mountain, so I told them to go on without me, as I wanted to stay at the top where there was good cellphone reception. I also wanted to be alone. Within about fifteen minutes, Fevvy phoned me back. All she could say was, 'Oh Fee, she's gone.' Ma had died just before Fevvy'd got to her. She had died when we were right on top of her mountain, the mountain she and our Dad had loved, the mountain she'd been so happy to hear we were going to climb. I was glad that I was by myself there, so that only the rocks around me could hear the long sad wail that I let out as I began to make my way down.

That was 1st July, 2003. Now, very early on Wednesday 5th October 2011, driving a group of sleepy teenagers to PE, I remembered how I had felt then, after Ma's death. Shock and disbelief had dominated the next few days. We couldn't believe that it was true, that Ma, whose strong personality had been a large part of our lives, was now gone. It seemed unbelievable, unreal. And as I drove, I realised that I now felt the same. There was the same level of shock and disbelief, the same feeling that this was just a weird dream and couldn't be real.

And yet there was a big difference. We had gained, not lost. It might be shocking and incredible and unreal, but nevertheless it was wonderful. We had gained a brother! The brother we had never had, the brother we would always have loved to have had. Oh goodness, I couldn't wait to get to Fevvy!

Chapter 19
Heather – The paper chase

How amazing that it seemed just another normal morning – the sun had come up, the birds were calling to each other and the city was waking up as it did every day.

I hugged my knees even more tightly to my chest and buried my face in the blanket covering them. My brain had started to spin with a hundred questions and emotions – thank goodness Fee would be arriving soon. Eventually I quietly climbed out of bed – sleeping late would be impossible and so, wrapped in my dressing gown, I headed back into the lounge to reread some of the documents Ralph had sent to our cousin Diane in America. I had printed them all up and had skimmed through them the previous day but now I needed to sit and reread everything before Fee arrived.

The Haven, where Ralph had been born, looked such a beautiful old stately home. I gently touched the photo – Ma had been there and suddenly I felt so grateful that such a beautiful place had existed.

The Haven, Yateley

I starting rereading the article Ralph had sent – it described how the house had been bought in 1945 by the Baptist Church for the purpose of helping *unmarried young women who found themselves pregnant*. I read that before this, during the war, the house had been used as a convalescent home for RAF officers. I read about how the Home for Mothers and Babies was established, and eventually I came to the place where the process of the babies being adopted was explained. One particular little paragraph caught my attention.

When the baby was three weeks old, the proposed adopters came to see it, and they returned to take it away at six weeks. Matron would put the baby in the arms of the adopting mother, saying that if she did not at once feel happy then this baby was not for her and no more would be said. This moment of joy was sometimes mixed with grief. One adopting mother wept for the natural mother whose baby she was taking, and had to be reassured by Matron that this was the very best thing for both mother and baby.

I screwed up my eyes and hugged the papers to my chest. What incredible heartache Ma must have gone through, but she must have believed that it was the best choice for her son and also for herself. I sat like that for some time. However had she coped with having to give her baby away?

I examined Ralph's adoption certificate again. It was dated 19th October 1949 – eleven days after his birth. So Ma's baby had been taken away from her so soon, just over a week after he was born.

I reread everything slowly – all Ralph's emails to Diane and then finally her one to Arthur when she had sent everything she had on to him. Oh my, this was all too amazing and I still felt I was about to awake from some crazy dream. My brain felt unable to concentrate on anything – I felt almost mentally paralysed and only able to think of Ma and Ralph and stare in bewilderment at the pages before me.

Adrian soon came padding through in his dressing gown and brought me a cup of coffee. Bathing and getting dressed would be a good idea, he gently advised.

As I had hoped, Fee arrived nice and early, at about eight, having left the farm at 5am. I knew she was bringing some music teenagers for an orchestra workshop, and that the girls would stay elsewhere in town but her own violin pupil would stay with us. She had already dropped him off at the orchestra rehearsal – poor fellow called David who I think I ignored the whole time he stayed with us. (Fortunately it turned out that Adrian had known his grandfather in his youth, so he and David chatted and watched TV together in the evenings while Fee and I lived with our eyes out on stalks.)

Adrian opened the big gate for Fee to drive her bakkie in and helped carry her bags upstairs to the front door. In one hand he had her usual small black suitcase of clothes but in the other he carried a blue case that I had not seen before. I stared at that case, knowing that if we were to get any answers they would probably be hidden somewhere inside it.

When Fee came up the stairs behind Adrian and walked towards me, I burst into a new flood of tears. She had left the farm so early that she had had no time to put on any makeup and so she just looked so incredibly like Ralph – she was the girl-version of our brother, though instead of his mop of curly hair, her long brown hair was in its usual plait. Oh goodness, it was just too much for my tired brain to handle. We hugged and cried and hugged and cried some more.

Then the real fun started. Looking back now, we always joke about that frenzied first week and that it was rather like the 1970s film *The Paper Chase*. The lounge became our headquarters and was literally strewn with papers, old photos and files for days on end and we just pored over and read everything we could possibly find that would slowly unravel the secret Ma had carried with her all her life.

Firstly we sat down with cups of coffee and Fee went over all that she had discovered whilst going through Ma's things the day before. We started with Ma's little old black photo albums and then Fee was already reaching into the suitcase again, and brought out Ma's old diary. I remembered it from long ago, an old brown book, almost A4 size, soft covered, with Ma's fluent blue handwriting inside it. Leafing quickly through the pages, Fee looked for what she wanted to show me next.

'I sat up last night reading this,' she said. 'I read it right through. Look, it never says anything, just goes on and on about life in London, until suddenly, here, look.' I gulped and moved even closer to her as she read aloud to me what Ma had written on the 18th June, about going to Yateley.

'Yateley, Fev,' Fee explained, though of course I knew. 'Yateley, where The Haven was.'

I felt the hairs on my arms rising and was quite overwhelmed thinking of young Ma all alone overseas, writing happy letters home to Granny – telling the truth of what she was doing, only leaving out certain incredible facts. 'Oh Ma,' I muttered for the hundredth time. Fee was nodding her head again and told me that she had felt just like I was now when she had come across this part of the diary in the middle of the night.

I needed to clear my head a bit, so we both went into the kitchen to make some more coffee. Laura was at work, and Adrian would be gone all day doing some repair work at my old house, so we didn't have to worry about him – I knew he realised that Fee and I needed time to talk and talk and find out all we could. When he left that morning, we had promised to tell him everything we discovered when he got home later and of course, for us having someone to tell was also very important as apart from Laura, Dawn and Fee's husband Rob, no-one else at all here knew anything about our brother finding us.

Clutching our fresh mugs of coffee we headed back into the lounge and once again settled down next to each other on the couch. Fee tried, in her calm and sensible way, to tell me about everything she had read and discovered from reading Ma's diary. She read aloud parts of it and then summarised the bits in between – Ma going to work in London, Ma going to the country to stay with Dr. Russell in Camberley, how she was treated almost as one of the family. Goodness it was nerve-racking waiting to hear something, just something that would let us know more of what really happened.

'Everything sounds perfectly normal,' Fee said, shaking her head as she read the daily events that Ma had recorded. 'All perfectly normal,' she said again, 'until...' and then I could hear the excitement building in her voice as she eventually stopped turning the pages and turned to look at me.

'Look here,' she said, pointing excitedly at the page where the writing had stopped on the 1st August and then started again on the 25th November – nearly four months missing!

I held my breath as I stared and stared at Ma's familiar handwriting, the pages blurring as my eyes filled with tears. Fee's voice was tight with emotion and excitement as she explained how she thought Ma must have used postcards or something like that when she pretended to lose her diary and so would just write quick, short messages home to her mother. Hectic stuff.

So much to take in. So much to understand. I started searching through the pile of papers on the coffee table.

'I remember reading something in the article that Ralph sent us on The Haven,' I said to Fee. 'Something about the length of time the young mothers needed to spend at The Haven and I am sure it was almost four months.' I hurriedly searched through the papers and found the article. I quickly scanned the pages. 'Yes, yes, see here,' I said, nearly bouncing off the couch, *'the girls were admitted eight weeks or more before their babies were due, by which time their expanding figures were difficult to conceal. During this period it was hoped they would become physically and mentally prepared for the birth and would have time to get to know the staff. They remained for about six weeks after the birth...'*

There it was. The girls were in the home for almost four months – the four months Ma had pretended to lose her diary. The four months during which Ma had given birth to Ralph. Fee and I shook our heads, leant back on the couch and shed fresh tears. We talked and talked and worked out that 25th November, the date on which the diary resumed, was nearly 7 weeks after Ma's baby was born. I wondered why she had stayed at The Haven so long, if Ralph was adopted on 19th October, but in all the emotion of the moment I didn't really have time to think about it.

Soon Fee was telling me about the other things she had found, and what they showed. There was so much to tell, she hardly knew where to start. I was feeling quite drained with emotion and could hear in Fee's voice that she was too.

I was still thinking about it all when she jumped up from the couch and started digging in her handbag, mumbling to herself that she wanted to phone George – George Irvine, our parents' old minister. What a good idea, I realised, a bubble of hope rising inside me – sensible Fee – he might have some answers or even advice. Perhaps Ma had told him her secret! He was a man whom our parents had both loved and who had been their good friend. Fee found her phone and I looked up George's number for her. I watched as she purposefully paced up and down behind the couch in our lounge, waiting for him to answer. George was the sort of person Ma might have confided in. He would have understood.

Holding my breath, I listened. George himself answered the phone and I heard Fee, for the very first time, telling someone outside of the family about our new brother. Once again my eyes brimmed with tears, while Fee continued to walk up and down, staring out of our big lounge window at the view across the valley, as she told the amazing story, stopping every once in a while to listen to what George was replying. Sadly, I soon realised that George was saying no, Ma had not told him anything. Fee talked a bit more and nodded her head at George's wise words, but I could see how disappointed she was. Where to look now? What we had hoped would be a possible answer, had been another dead end.

After the photo albums and the diary, the next thing Fee pulled out of the blue suitcase was our grandfather's old satchel, full of papers. I remembered that brown leather satchel, remembered seeing it in Ma's bottom drawer long ago. I hadn't seen it since we packed up Ma's things after she had died in 2003. I watched closely as Fee took out various letters, laying them on the coffee table and saying we must read them, but first she wanted to show me Granny's little address book.

I didn't remember ever having seen it before, a slim pocket book, covered in soft pink leather. Fee flipped through the pages, talking non-stop of course, and tapping the pages to stress a point, and so, gradually, I made sense of what she was telling me.

She showed me the page where Granny had pasted in the letterhead from the secretarial college, showing that Ma's trip overseas had been planned by at least as early as November 1948. There were Ma's initials, 'D.R.W.', written in Granny's distinctive handwriting I remembered so well, along with two London addresses, one dated January 1950. This 1950 address Fee said was the very one that Ma had given Granny in the last letter in the diary. And even as she showed this to me,  her voice rose with excitement as she realised that the 'Mrs Cunningham' of the other address must be Ma's landlady, 'Mrs C.', who Ma had written about so often in her letters to Granny. Only now, having read the diary in the night, did she realize who 'Mrs C.' was. This realisation wasn't terribly important in our search for the truth, but it was as if Ma's past was coming alive to us – we were getting to know some of the characters in this long ago story. Every detail felt as if we were slowly putting a puzzle together – each little piece fitting into place to finally, hopefully, give us the finished picture.

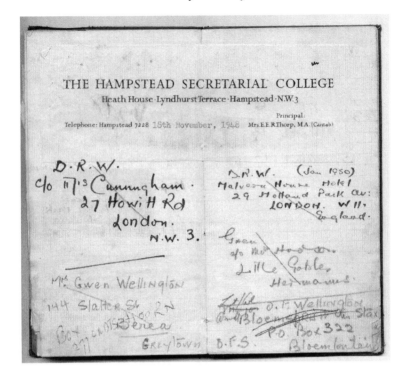

THE HAMPSTEAD SECRETARIAL COLLEGE
Heath House · Lyndhurst Terrace · Hampstead · N.W.3

Principal:
Telephone: Hampstead 7228 15th November, 1948 Mrs. E.E.R.Thorp, M.A. (Cantab)

Fee broke into my thoughts and sounded even more excited as she rummaged in the suitcase again and came up with a small leather pouch, which contained Ma's 1948 passport. I took the passport from her and looked happily at the photo of Ma. I loved seeing her looking so young and pretty.

But that isn't what Fee wanted to show me. She waved the leather passport wallet at me and passed it to me open, pointing to an address written on the inside of the flap. I recognized Ma's handwriting of course, as I looked at what was written. Fee leant closer and said excitedly she'd only just realised, only realised right now, that the address on the inside of the wallet was the address of the Hampstead Secretarial College. I caught her excitement and what she was getting at – this meant that the college address must have been the very first London address that Ma was sure of, and so had used it when labelling her passport wallet probably well before leaving South Africa. It finally proved to us that the main purpose of Ma's getting her passport was to study in London.

I looked at Granny's little address book lying open on the coffee table in front of us and carefully read all the other addresses below the Secretarial College letterhead. Fee leant over as well and read aloud from the book but stopped abruptly when she got to 'Mrs Gwen Wellington'. 'Look, Fev, this is Aunty Fluffy! This reminds me, I wanted to ask you – do you think Ma ever told Aunty Fluffy her secret?'

Quite possibly, I thought, for Ma had been very fond of her sister-in-law. And then I shook my head, not from amazement but because I was sure. 'No, Fee,' I said. 'No. I remember something Aunty Fluffy once said. She wouldn't have said it if she had known about Ma's son.'

It had happened long ago, when I was still a teenager. I had been there one day when Aunty Fluffy was visiting us, and had heard her thanking Ma for always welcoming her sons with open arms whenever they came to visit. (At various times, most of them had come to stay with us for a while, while either working or studying in Port Elizabeth.) Ma had been saying how she loved having them to stay. Aunty Fluffy had then jokingly said to Ma, 'Ruthie, if you wanted a son so much, you should have had one of your own!'

I told this to Fee, and we were sure. Aunty Fluffy could never have teased so light-heartedly if she had known about Ma's painful secret. Again we shed tears as we realised how Aunty

Fluffy's words must unintentionally have hurt Ma. She had indeed had a son of her own, but had lost him forever. Imagine Ma having to deal with little incidents like this throughout her life, without ever being able to say anything to anyone. At this realisation I again descended into saying 'Good Lord!' over and over, as I stumbled off to fetch more tissues.

Chapter 20
Heather – Writing to Ralph

'How are we going to reply to him?' we seemed to say over and over again to each other that mad morning. Knowing that we needed to e-mail our *brother* for the first time, with our minds still reeling in shock, was adding more urgency to our search for clues. How does one say hello to a brother you never knew you had, have never met and don't know at all? There was still so much to talk about and find out, so many unanswered questions, so many things to read and digest. What also made the task doubly difficult was our emotions. This was the most incredible thing that had ever happened to us and we felt almost mentally paralysed – stunned – by it.

Fee was looking through more of the papers that were in our grandfather's satchel, muttering about a brown envelope she had seen the day before, and wanted to show me. She had already read to me bits out of Granny's letters to Ma, especially the 1950 one that proved to us that Granny knew absolutely nothing about the baby Ma had given up just a few months before.

Fee found what she had been looking for and held it up, nodding her head triumphantly at me – an envelope with Ma's writing on the cover. Fee explained that she remembered Ma writing this for one of her grandchildren who had been asking her to tell them 'about your trip to England, Granny, when you were young'. Fee said she'd been there that day visiting our parents, and remembered Ma writing this for 'Baby Heather' (her daughter named after me), perhaps in about the year 2000. Fee said she had taken it home to give to her when she came home from boarding school. Heather had been particularly close to her Granny.

'LOOK what it says, Fev!' Fee was saying excitedly.

Together we read the words Ma had scrawled on the envelope.

Pushed out of college after 3 months as I had worked for 2 years already – got temp job behind St Paul's cathedral in Smithfield Market with firm of lawyers and used to go to the Old Bailey with my boss quite often.

That part I already knew. Ma had told me about going to the secretarial college and not being there long before being allowed to leave with the necessary certificate – they'd said that she already knew all they could teach her. But the next bit had my eyes out on stalks:

Got too hot in London in 1949 heatwave and went to the country for 6 months as Drs receptionist, and learnt to deliver babies!!! Then back to London for the winter, and joined 600 group of companies in North Acton – sec. to the M.D. Boo worked in the Advertising Branch in White City.

Fee explained to me that the 600 group of companies was the George Cohen group, that Ma had written about in the diary. Our Dad, whose nickname was Boo, also worked there, and that is how they met. Fee picked up Granny's little pink address book again and showed me the page where Granny had pasted a letterhead from Ma's work into it.

But of course Ma's workplace and her meeting our Dad wasn't the thing that really got our attention – the lines *Got too hot in London in 1949 heatwave and went to the country for 6 months as Drs receptionist, and learnt to deliver babies!!! Then back to London for the winter...* had us gasping, but also snorting with mirth – too *hot* in London for someone from Africa? This is how Ma explained her time away from London. Perhaps she realised that no one would read the diary carefully enough – I had never bothered to read it at all – to see that she was *never* the doctor's receptionist – but now, of course, Fee had read every single word of it last night, and was leaning forward and closer to me on the couch, urgently telling me that before Ma left for the country, she had been insisting in her letters to her mother that England *wasn't* really hot at all.

And as for learning *to deliver babies*! How we wished we had asked Ma more about that! If we had really asked, and been really interested, and been really sympathetic listeners, perhaps she would have told us her secret. Oh how I wished she had, but of course, she couldn't. I would anyway most likely have thought that my always sharp-minded mother had finally gone a bit crazy. And also, if she had told us, how would we ever have found him? We would not have known his adopted name and we didn't use the internet when Ma was still alive. Ma was always such a wise woman and she must have realised all these things. Oh my, it must have been so terribly, terribly hard for her.

I picked up Granny's little address book and started slowly paging through it, determined to find something. I looked again at all the addresses Fee had shown me and told me about – the Secretarial College, as well as Ma's various London addresses – and kept reading and looking at the many many entries. I was about to turn a page when a name caught my eye and I suddenly realised what I was staring at.

'Goodness, Fee, look at this, it says Dr. and Mrs Russell, Northcote House, Blackwater, Camberley. This has to be the Russell family that Ma stayed with.' I could feel a lump in my throat and swallowed hard as I passed the book to Fee.

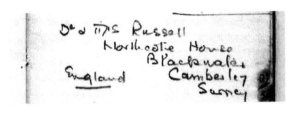

Fee stared at it and then starting nodding her head and tapping the address. 'Oh yes, yes, it is,' she said excitedly. 'I remember this from Ma's diary.' She hurriedly picked up the diary and found the page she was looking for. 'Yes, here it is. On the 25th November when Ma left The Haven, went to London and then returned to the Russells for the weekend, she heads that day with the title: Northcote House – Blackwater. I thought it must be their address, but wasn't sure.'

The way Granny had written Dr. and Mrs meant something too – it meant she had not known the Russells at all, she didn't know their first names – they couldn't be distant relatives, or people Granny had helped Ma find.

Sometime during all this I realised that although Fee said she'd eaten a sandwich in the bakkie on the way to PE, I hadn't eaten at all. Food had been the furthest thing from my mind, but now I realised that perhaps the odd feeling in my tummy wasn't only from emotion. Fee followed me through to the kitchen, still clutching Ma's diary as she continued to talk about Ma and the Russells, pointing to pages and dates as she tossed ideas about. She pointed out how the pen carbon book had a big printed page number on each right-hand page, and how Ma herself had written the left-hand page numbers in with a fine red pen. I stopped buttering the toast and I looked at those red numbers in Ma's slightly quavery handwriting – from when she was old and ill – and my eyes opened wide. Goodness me, I *knew* this pen – I could still see the scene quite clearly in my mind of Ma sitting in her chair during the last year of her life, the year after our Dad had died, wearing her oxygen tube, looking at accounts that had come in and marking them off as paid or unpaid with a *red felt-tipped pen* – with this same pen, and with a slight shake in her writing. Good Lord!

I realised what this meant, and battled to speak through my tears as I told Fee. Ma must have been rereading her diary and marking the pages during that last year of her life. There were one or two places in the diary where dates or a comment had been added in the same red ink. Fee showed me the entry for 29th July, where Ma had added the year, and had written '22nd birthday' next to the date, and then she was suddenly paging back to July 17th and pointing out to me how Ma had been reading *Pride and Prejudice* when she was staying with the Russells.

'Oh Fev,' she said, 'she asked me to get her this book! I fetched my old red copy from home for her. She must have asked for it because of this diary.' We agreed that in her old age, in that last year when she was alone, Ma must have been re-living in her mind that time in 1949 when she gave up her only son. No wonder she was so incredibly broken and sad!

Now we knew for sure that she had grieved not only for our father but also for Ralph. Oh goodness, I think we forgot all about the toast – well, I certainly don't remember eating it and we probably left it half buttered in the kitchen as this realisation sunk in. Our strong, sensible mother had cried so much that last year of her life and I remember worrying about her almost extreme grief for such a normally strong woman – now I fully understood that it had been a double sorrow, a double sense of loss. Imagine knowing that you were going to die, and that you would never find out what had happened to the child you had given away so many years ago. We both cried and wished that we had understood Ma better... if only Ma could somehow have explained things to us.

And yet, in spite of our deep sadness for Ma, there was also a growing sense of joy inside me. The feeling seemed to start very small, a little excited bubble, and slowly it swelled and got bigger and bigger as the day went on. It seemed to be starting to replace the knotted, muddled confused emotions of before. Imagine having a brother! We had always just been the two of us sisters, very close friends. Now suddenly there was this person on the other side of the world who looked like us, was part of us, and wanted to make contact with us. It seemed to be just the most wonderful thing we could ever have imagined.

It must have been sometime in the early afternoon when at last we decided we were ready – well, as ready as one can ever be to contact an unknown brother for the first time – and together we went through to the study and sat down at the computer.

Our small neat study contained two desks and several overloaded bookshelves, and its walls were lined with photos from various travels that Adrian and I had enjoyed together, as well as cases of butterflies I had collected when I was young. But now, of course, we saw none of these things. Goodness. I stared at the computer screen – my mind almost a total blank as to how to start.

It took us the whole afternoon. There was so much to tell him, yet what do you say? How do you tell everything in one e-mail? We couldn't, of course, so decided to tell just what we thought essential in this first correspondence. I typed and Fee sat on a chair next to me – we both suggested things to say – we wrote, deleted many times and wrote more until we felt satisfied with what we had said. We looked through the albums again and scanned some of the photos of young Ma so that he could see what his mother had looked like. Also, we realised we'd better attach a photo of ourselves – *we* knew that he looked 'just like us', but *he* didn't know this yet.

Finding a photo of us together would have been a problem up until a few weeks ago. There had been no recent photos of the two of us together at all – none had been taken for about twenty years or more, but luckily, just three weeks ago I had gone up to Fee's farm with Dawn, and she had taken a lovely picture of the two of us in the veld. We decided to send this to him.

I will never forget the incredible nervous excitement I felt when we had finally finished writing and re-writing, had attached all the pictures, and it was time for me to click 'send'. Up until the very last moment before this e-mail was sent, we would still be just the two of us – but once sent – we would become three!

From: Heather
To: Ralph Wellington
Sent: 5 October, 2011
Subject: From Fiona and Heather

Dear Ralph (Martyn),
Hi – wow – Hi – wow again. We are speechless—

Chapter 21
The fatted calf

S o here I was, about to read the email from my sisters. My mind flashed back to when, as a little boy of twelve, I first made the decision to find my real mother and family. I had viewed the quest as an almost Arthurian journey, being inspired by a story of terrible deeds in a far-off land and of a distressed young maiden forced to take an epic journey into the unknown.

> *It was the closing of the day:*
> *She loos'd the chain and down she lay;*
> *The Broad stream bore her far away,*
> *The Lady of Shalott.*

The painting of the girl in the boat that had hung in my mother's house, Waterhouse's painting, was the image of this verse that I had carried in my mind for so many years. As a young boy I had been heading into the unknown myself, to find a world in which I would belong. Over the years, through many obstacles, the intensity of that picture had never faded. On more than one occasion it had been the inspiration that had kept me going on the quest, leading me to this fateful afternoon, October 5th 2011.

After this single click of the mouse, my life was to change forever.

From: Heather
To: Ralph Wellington
Sent: 5 October, 2011
Subject: From Fiona and Heather

Dear Ralph (Martyn),
Hi – wow – Hi – wow again. We are speechless – well, not really, as we have not stopped talking since yesterday morning when cousin Arthur contacted us about you. First of all we are surprised, amazed and totally delighted to discover a brother we had no idea existed. Ma kept your birth a complete and total secret from everybody – even from her own mother. (We can tell this from old letters, especially Ma's letters written to Granny in the form of a diary when she was in England.) Some of what you have been told is not correct and over time we will try to sort it all out for you.
We are sitting together at the computer. I, Heather, am typing, and Fiona has come to visit for a few days. We are feeling extremely emotional. Discovering this about Ma has enabled us to understand her so much better. The thing that has struck us most forcefully is a sudden understanding of something that was sometimes difficult for us to cope with. Ma was totally wonderful and gave us the most loving and stable childhood, but after we each married, we experienced the same problem. She battled to let us go... and we now know why. Letting you go affected

her for the rest of her life and it was a secret she had to carry alone.

We have a clearly labelled photo album that shows the dates of her boat trip to England. In the album it says 22nd January to 11th February, 1949. This means that she may not even have known she was pregnant when she set sail. But it does mean that you were conceived in South Africa, before she left. Diane's ideas about your father may be right. Judging by some things Ma said to us when she was still alive, 'Luke' could indeed have been your father, though something happened between them that caused her to resent him for the rest of her life.

There is so much we want to tell you and will. We just wanted to send a few photos to you and say hello. We are so astounded at all this; it is just amazing.

One thing we want to say now is that the story of Ma meeting our Dad on the boat coming home is totally untrue as this refers to some other relatives (Maggie Wellington, our grandfather's sister, and her husband Tom). Ma and our Dad married on the 2nd June, 1951, in Oxford at the church of St. Michael at the North Gate. Six months later, they came to South Africa. Fiona was born in 1954 and Heather in 1956. There is much to tell you but we will go slowly as catching up with 50-odd years will take time.

You need to know how wonderful your mother was. She was a brave and compassionate woman who was a wonderful mother to us and a friend to a great many people. We are sure she would have loved to have been a mother to you. She died in 2003, a year after our father. They had been devoted to each other for 51 years. Ma was born on the 29th July, 1927. She grew up at Healdtown where, as you know, her father was Governor of the Mission Institution. She went to boarding school in Queenstown where she became Head of the Hostel and did very well. She went to a secretarial college in Port Elizabeth and then worked for a couple of years before going to England. She wrote the following for one of our children who asked her about her time in England – 'I got a temporary job behind St. Paul's Cathedral in Smithfield Market with a firm of lawyers and had to go to the old Bailey with my boss quite often. Got too hot in London in the 1949 heatwave and went to the country for six months as a doctor's receptionist. Then back to London for the winter and joined 600 Group of Companies as Secretary to the MD.'

We want to send this off to you now although there is still so much to say. Wow – we have a brother! (I, Heather, have been walking around for the last day shaking my head and saying 'Good Lord!' all the time.)

Love

Fiona and Heather

It is almost an impossibility to describe how reading four lines of type can have such a profound effect on one's mind-set, a totally life-changing event encapsulated in four sentences. I say this because that is as far as I got when first reading my sisters' e-mail. I became so overwhelmed with joy, that, for a few minutes, I could read no further. I was a Wellington!

Across the top, in a neat row were photographs, the thumbnail images ready for viewing. The first appeared to be a young girl; it was old, black and white: it had to be my mother. I opened the picture, tears streaming down my face as I realised what I was seeing. This was mother travelling to England on the ship in 1949, smiling and happy. Here was my *real* Lady of Shalott – I had finally found her. The image of the tormented soul was here replaced by one of gladness and joy. Mother had come to England, happy and radiant. I cannot describe the sense of relief and joy I encountered here. I guess I already knew this really from the shipping list but it had not completely sunk in and this picture laid the ghost of the original story for good. This was my mother. I was in this picture too, tiny and yet to be discovered.

Ma on the R.M.M.V. Capetown Castle

I returned to the text, reread the wonderful first sentences and continued as best I could, trying to take in all the information Heather and Fiona had sent to me. Fifty years I had waited for this and now reading the entire text, I had slightly recovered and was enjoying every revelation, despite the tears that spilled onto my keyboard. Mother had been a wonderful, strong mother to her children and a loved and respected person, but I really was the skeleton in her cupboard. I had been kept a total secret.

So many questions were answered on that day and by the time I had read the complete e-mail I knew I truly had become Ralph, a brother, accepted and loved by sisters and the extended Wellington family. Finally, I knew who I was.

I opened the remaining pictures and the revelations kept coming: there was mother in 1950, she truly was my mother by that time, but I just stared and stared. The most amazing thing of all was the family likeness, for here was my daughter Abi.

'Wow, this is just incredible, amazing!'

I was talking to myself by this time. And my mother was

sitting in a small boat, happy and smiling. How did my sisters know to send this picture from all they had? I am sure they could not have known what an effect it would have, how it represented so clearly the end of my searching.

This was followed by mother as a girl with her brothers, my uncles, immaculate and standing proud in their military uniforms. Frank, Alex and Ralph (pronounced Raif, the caption said). What stories was I to hear about their world?

The last picture attached was the most wonderful of all. Here were my sisters and I could tell in an instant why the photos of Abi and me had had such an effect on them. The strength of the Wellington genes was undeniable; they looked just like me! Two lovely girls who between them shared all the family features I had for so many years longed to see. Looking at Fiona was like looking at myself with a plait!

My sisters – and they loved me – the quest was complete.

I read through their email so many times that by the time I was ready to produce any coherent sort of reply, I almost knew its contents by heart. I read it on my own, I read it with Helen, I even read it out loud to myself trying to take in all it said. Cousin Arthur's call and emails had obviously sent my sisters into 'research mode' themselves and I had a mental picture of them opening drawers and cupboards, poring over old, neglected family letters and diaries, searching for clues which may have been left hidden in the contents. I particularly liked the story of Mother going to the country to escape the London heat of 1949. No lies were told; she had simply left out a lot of details! I imagined Fiona and Heather rereading all this now in a slightly different light. I thought again about what a complete shock this must have been.

By the time I was ready to send my reply, my first ever message to my sisters, it was nearly midnight. I had decided to keep it short and not too full of questions, although I had a million to ask. They could all come later and the greatest joy for me at that moment was that there would be a 'later'.

From: Mart Bradley
To: Heather
Sent: 5 October, 2011
Subject: RE: From Fiona and Heather

Dear Fiona and Heather
To say I'm over the moon would be the understatement of the decade. Receiving your email today marks the end of a journey I thought I would never complete. I started trying to trace my family over 40 years ago and on several occasions having drawn complete blanks, almost gave up

totally. Now, with the journey over and such a warm and loving response from you both and all the Wellington family members, today is one of the happiest days of my life.

I read your wonderful email and got as far as your descriptions of how mother 'battled to let you go' and how carrying the secret had affected her entire life and burst into tears. Only you two can really understand and share the depth of emotion I am feeling as I write this. I still find it hard to really believe I'm writing to my sisters. Thank you, thank you so much for welcoming me so warmly to the family.

I'm so glad that you say that the discovery has helped you to understand our mother more. The photographs you have sent are wonderful and answer so many questions. Seeing her on the boat radiant and happy is quite amazing. Not surprisingly, she is beautiful – I always knew in my heart she would be. I can see so much of my daughter Abigail there. Abi will be home at the weekend – she will be speechless too! Perhaps the best of all though is the picture of the two of you – my sisters. Fifty years of knowing no true relatives has been a hard road.

I will email you again tomorrow when my head recovers and I remember all the host of things I want to say.

I end this in exactly the same way you ended your email – wow, I have two wonderful sisters. I will continue to walk around in a daze in the morning!!

After sending this, I was in no mood for ending what was truly one of my life's greatest days. I was on a tremendous high and wandered around the house occasionally pinching myself to check that I was not actually within a particularly cruel dream. I returned to the computer in the early hours and opened the

1820settlers.com site. I wanted to know more about my new family, and sleep wasn't going to get in the way! I needed to know why the family was in South Africa in the first place, which meant delving into the history of the Wellington family on grandfather's side in Cornwall. So many questions, so much joy... Finally I fell into bed, happy but exhausted.

The next morning, 6th October, I woke up as Ralph Wellington for the first time. I was part of a very large and loving extended family who all lived far away in South Africa and who had welcomed me in a way I had never dared dream possible. The quest was complete, the contact made and the skeleton had quit the family cupboard.

From: Heather
To: Ralph Wellington
Sent: 6 October, 2011
Subject: From Heather

Dear Ralph, (or should we call you Martyn – let us know?)
Our minds are still in such a turmoil – we can't sleep and all we think about is you and Ma and everything. It's just so so amazing and the fact that we had no idea just adds to the 'freakoutness' of the whole thing. It's just incredible and I get terribly emotional. Fee (Fiona) has taken her violin pupil off for a lesson and she will also write to you later but I thought I would send a little about myself and kids and some more photos.
On Tuesday when Fee phoned to say she had received your photo and I asked, with trepidation, what you looked like, her emotional reply was – 'just like us'. Well, I just starting sobbing. Wow it's just so amazing and of course, Abigail is just like all our kids – so so many likenesses it's

frightening. Both my children have been told and Fee's youngest, also called Heather, was told today and the rest will be told over the next few days. (Fee has four children and I have two. Fee's eldest, Shirley, is away in America with her husband and returns to London, where they live, on Sunday – Fee will tell you more.) The kids who know are delighted and find it totally fascinating. After all, this normally only happens in books!

Now about me, your baby sister. After school I studied accountancy at Rhodes and then worked up in Johannesburg for a personnel company. I married my first husband, Gavin Hamilton, in 1978. We had two children, Laura born in 1982 and Keith, born in 1984. Gavin died in 2000 from pancreatic cancer – he died 3 months after diagnosis and it was just too shocking... I am just giving you the abridged version of my life.

Ma and Dad had moved to a retirement village near me by this stage and I found their support incredible. They needed me and I badly needed them. Ma's health was failing as she had broken her hip and this had put a severe strain on her heart and lungs – she suddenly needed to go on oxygen. Her heart was weak from having had Rheumatic fever as a child and her lungs were also not very good. I saw them often as I took them their supper each evening. Those last years were very special to all of us. Dad died in 2002 and Ma just never recovered from his loss. She cried a lot during this time and now I am sure she cried for you as well.

You will discover from us and from the rest of the family, that our Ma was just amazing. I think what she went through in having to give you up gave her incredible empathy for other people. She never criticised. She opened her heart and house to anyone lonely or in need of love. There was often an extra person at mealtimes and on Christmas eve she would have an open house and would hang lots of tiny gifts on the Christmas tree so that each person could take just a little something home with them. Anyway, I lived on my own with my kids until 2007 when I met my present husband, Adrian Oberholzer, also widowed. We married after a year and have been extremely happy. He is a wonderful, caring, kind and gentle man. Reminds me a lot of my father. He was an air-traffic controller for many years and got his pilot's licence as well, before going into business. He retired early and moved to Port Elizabeth after his wife's death at the end of 2006. Ma would have loved him, I know.

I have worked as Bursar at a local primary school for the past 18 years. I love the people and of course, I get all the school holidays each year. If I need extra time off to travel with Adrian, it's never a problem and I want to keep working as long as possible as I just love it so – think I'm like Ma – she loved working and did so as long as she could. (I, like Ma, did not work when my kids were young.)

Lots and lots of love to you, Helen and Abi (you will have to come and meet us all sometime.)

Christmas 2003: David, Douglas, Shirley, Heather – Fee's kids – then Laura and Keith – mine

The photo of the six cousins was incredible. I couldn't believe it wasn't Abi sitting there second from right, but of course it was Heather's daughter, Laura!

Dear Heather and Fiona,
I think I know exactly how you are feeling! I tried to do some work this morning (I still do a little from home) and had to redo the whole thing as my concentration level was little above zero today. The 'freakoutness' (what a great word) played on my mind as well – I just can't really believe what has happened in the last week.
The fact that we all look the same I guess is not surprising but still just amazing to take in. I am finding it really mind-blowing with the opening of each picture. I know I have a school photo somewhere where I look exactly like your son, Heather – I must find it. But the most incredible likeness is Abi and Laura. The picture you have sent with

this email of all the children made me just gasp – it *is* Abi
in the photo. Helen almost fell over as well when we put
it up on full-screen – wow!! I'm emailing them to Abi later
– she really will fall over!

I think the best thing is for me to try to get sensible and
tell you about myself, so here goes:

I was adopted almost immediately after I was born – 19th
October the adoption cert says – and taken home by my
adoptive parents...

Mum and Dad were loving and kind and instilled me
with a set of values which have served me well all my life.
Mum died when I was in my 20s. Dad remarried and
spent the last few years of his life in New Zealand, where
he died in 1999. We last saw him in 1991 when we were
living in Australia and visited NZ for a couple of weeks.
Most of my life has been spent playing music of one sort
or another. I played mainly on the folk music circuit in the
UK and Europe – guitar and concertina – and made quite
a lot of recordings in the late 70s and early 80s – it will be
fun for you to hear those!! Helen sings in two choirs
and has been really busy this year with rehearsals and
various live singing events. I guess Abi is the real star now
– she is a very good singer, flute player and guitarist – I'll
try to get some of her sounds to you as well.

I love being called Ralph so please do! – that's what my
birth certificate says and I hope I shall always be Ralph to
you and the Wellington Family. I'm sure mother named
me after her elder brother and I am proud to have the
name. I especially like the fact that you pronounce it Raif
– as in Vaughan-Williams, my absolutely favourite
composer. Oh wow – I can't even get through this email
without having to stop and decide whether it's all real or
not!!

I'm sure I've left out lots I meant to say but as you said –
not too much at a time – it's all so amazing my head's not
working that well!!

*Left to right: 1952 family – this is me with my adoptive parents
Gerald and Dorothy Bradley at Old Vicarage Farm, Dovercourt;
Dovercourt 1952; Family 1995*

In between writing long emails to each other, some short ones
were exchanged too:

From: Mart Bradley
To: Heather
Sent: 7 October, 2011
Subject: RE: From Heather

Hi Heather and Fiona
All your emails and pictures came through OK. Hope
mine got there with so many attachments.
It's the middle of the night here – I just can't sleep. Had a
real good cry – I feel so happy.
much love
Ralph

From: Heather
To: Ralph
Sent: 7 October, 2011
Subject: Re: From Heather

Oh wow oh goodness. We can't sleep either. Fee was up at
the crack of dawn and typing to you which we will send
later today – more about 1949 – such fascinating stuff.
Lots and lots of love, we also keep crying – it's good. Your
letter was wonderful – we just loved it. More later.
Lots love again
Fee and Fev (Heather, Feather, Fevver, Fev – happened
when I was very little and has stuck with the family.)

From: Ralph
To: Heather
Subject: Re: From Heather
Date: 7 October, 2011

Hi Heather and Fiona (can I call you Fee and Fev – that
sounds so good)
I've just found some more pictures of Abi. You can see
how much she looks like Laura.
More to follow later
With love
Ralph

Dear Ralph

Fee and Fev is what we have always called each other and what we would love you as our brother to call us.

Thank you so much for your reply to Heather's letter last night. So interesting, lovely to see more photos. We enjoyed it very much. Oh my goodness.

Of course Ma was musical too, and played the piano as one of her matric subjects. Some of us are too.

Going back to 1949. One thing Fevvy and I have been discussing is that we must let you know what we have found out about that year when you were born...

Hi Fee and Fev

This is getting more and more fantastic and even better than a book! We have a TV series called *Who Do You Think You Are?* – this is better than anything they have done!

It is wonderful and quite amazing that you have kept all

the diaries and mother's writings. Mother must have been such a strong, calm and totally together person to write: *I had made arrangements to go down to see someone in Yateley today and certainly couldn't have chosen a more perfect day* and *Having got my diary back, I had better make use of it. I decided that I'd go back to London for the winter* – wonderful, totally 'ordinary' statements – and such different meanings in context now! I am developing a great admiration for the way in which mother came through what must have been a very difficult period in her life – especially if she herself didn't know she was carrying me until after she had left South Africa. Looking again at the timings of the voyage and the dates, I suspect this is probably the case. What do you think? The way she wrote about what was happening in her life without ever telling an untruth – wow...

We have some very good friends who have lived in Camberley for years. I'm sure they will be up for researching into Jen Russell. If anyone can trace her, they will. It would be very interesting to meet up if she is still alive. I can't find anything about Northcote House, but will have a look next time I'm up that way. Abi is stationed at Aldershot at present (much safer than Afghanistan last year), which is only just down the road from Yateley and Blackwater. Can't wait to get up there and see what I can find out, but of course it is possible that the house has gone.

Dr. Russell doesn't seem to have been involved in the daily running of The Haven – another doctor is mentioned. I've found an online history written by a member of staff, where most of the staff seem to be mentioned by name – it's interesting reading. I've attached a few more pictures of The Haven as it was a superb building. Unfortunately, like so many other old mansions here, it was demolished!

Now it is later – just gone 10 at night. My very best friend (we were at school together when we were 14 in Dartford) and his lady have just been here for a meal – they were completely blown away by the whole thing. Dave was best man at our wedding in 1977 and knew my adoptive parents very well. He has known the story for years. He looked at the picture of you two and almost fell over! Abi is also here for the evening. She came home for the night and sends all her love to you both. She is amazed at just how much she really does look like Heather and Laura. She is thrilled to bits by the whole thing and thinks we ought to be getting on a plane tomorrow!!

With love to you both

Ralph

Dear Ralph

It's Fee up very early again. Once I'm conscious my eyes just fly open and there is no more chance of sleep! I run to Fevvy's computer, and, with the time difference between us, there is often... Fevvy's door is opening and here she is with me now too! It is just after 6 on Saturday morning. What I was saying was that with the time difference between us there is often an e-mail waiting for us in the morning, which is very exciting!! And there is one!!

So this is now from both of us!

Happy Birthday!!!

with lots of love from your new sisters!!

What a wonderful day!

Thank you for your wonderful letter.

We are so happy that we are sharing in your discovery of what happened around the time of your birth... But from your e-mail and the Haven attachment, we have discovered something more. You say in your letter: 'Dr. Russell doesn't seem to have been involved in the daily running of The Haven – another doctor is mentioned.' BUT we are female Poirots, and on closer reading have discovered otherwise. Note this from the article:

*The expert medical care which has been given to the girls through the years has helped considerably to achieve this record. Dr. John Price, is, and has been a great friend of the work since early 1953, as was the late **Dr. W. R. Russell before him**. They have both taken a keen interest in the welfare of the girls and staff spiritually, medically and socially, as well as serving on the Adoption Case Committee as medical adviser. Dr. John Price is always very considerate and helpful – never failing to come quickly when called, bringing with him an atmosphere of calm reassurance. How good God has been, and how He has blessed the work!*

This freaked us out, to know that Ma stayed at the home of the actual doctor of the place for a month before the time, and for at least a weekend afterwards. Go, Ma!! In her photo album we have found a few small pictures taken in April 1950 of Ma and Jennifer at Northcote House. She obviously loved these people and went back there for a weekend. So sad that Dr. Russell died in 1953. So glad that you have good friends in Camberley who might be able to trace Jen for you (and for us!!!) Thanks for the awesome photos of The Haven – what a beautiful place – and we love what the article says. As for the photo of Abi – as usual, wow and wow again. She is so like our kids, it is uncanny...

And we say, YES PLEASE, come soon!! Any time! What about Christmas in South Africa? Lovely and warm here... **Any time you like we would love you to come**. All the cousins (too many!) say they want to kill the fatted calf!

Fevvy and I have been so happy to be together this week on this most AMAZING voyage of discovery. We two sisters have always been very close, we are each other's best friends, which we have recently come to appreciate more than ever. And NOW to discover you has just blown us away.

Today is quite an emotional day for us thinking of our Ma this day 62 years ago. Oh my goodness. We just keep saying to ourselves, just imagine. We know how beautiful our own babies were, and we can't imagine how terrible it must have been for Ma to give up her beautiful baby boy. It makes us happy though to read about The Haven and what a lovely, dignified, well-run and Christian place it was.

Lots of love, and
Happy Birthday!!!
Have a wonderful 62nd birthday!
Love, Fee and Fev

Hi Fee and Fev
Wonderful to get your birthday email this morning. I've just got in after a very long day, ending up at the Victorian Steam Fair. This was to be my special birthday treat but after getting two sisters no other birthday present comes close!

Thanks so much for your birthday wishes, so thoughtfully sent so they were there when I logged-on this morning. I had so many birthday emails from my new-found family, I think it was probably the best birthday I've ever had. I'm feeling very blessed although I too have been thinking of that day 62 years ago – I can see it now in a totally different context, of course. I sat quietly outside in the moonlight just now, thinking of how Ma must have coped with the whole situation – what an amazing lady. Brilliant that you spotted Doctor Russell's details on the Haven info. Poirots you certainly are! Helen and I can't believe we missed it, although we're not thinking very straight at present. That certainly answers a whole heap of questions posed by Ma's diaries. As you say, she must have developed a real love for the family and if we can trace Jennifer Russell there could be a lot more come to light through her memories. The Haven really looks to have been a beautiful place and it is a great shame it went the same way as so many of England's grand houses. We would love to come and see you. In fact, I can't wait to see you both and your families. I just want to be there now to give you both the biggest hugs in the world. Abi is leaving the army after 6 years and will be finished sometime in December. She can't wait to meet all her new cousins. Could you possibly cope with us descending on you at the end of the year? There are so many places I am longing to see: Graaff-Reinet, Healdtown, Hogsback and of course, where you two live, not to mention the entire country!!

The response I got from Heather to this plan was very enthusiastic: 'Yes yes you must all come... what a Christmas present for us all – oh it is just so incredible.'

As we began initial planning, however, a major problem arose. Abi's official leaving date was 1st March 2012 but, as she had accrued lots of leave, we were all under the impression that her actual leaving date was towards the end of December. What we didn't realise until later was that she had to account for this time as practical working towards possible jobs in Civvy St and she couldn't use it for holiday. This meant the earliest we could all travel would be March 2012.

I had begun to imagine Christmas in South Africa with my sisters and waiting until March seemed horrendous. Another three whole months, how could I possibly cope with that! And then I started to think rationally... Actually, I had waited for this for a mere fifty years. This objective had been the most important thing in my life for just about as long as I could remember, so what difference was an extra few months going to make?!

We soon realised that March would be perfect and, with very few restrictions on our travel, we could be in South Africa for enough time to really get to know the new family. We all agreed that it really would be the trip of a lifetime and planning needed to get off the ground sooner rather than later.

We were now in the process of discovering more and more about each other, albeit via e-mail, and the more I discovered, the more I loved these people. (My sisters were also in the process of recovering from shock, of course.) And now meeting up became the thing I wished for more than anything else. I would never meet Ma but I could come to know her through her daughters. She was the fundamental influence throughout their upbringing and, more than anyone else, was responsible for who they were as individuals. Now to finally meet up was just a wonderful idea, made all the better in that the first invitation had come from Fee and Fev. The more I thought about it, the more it became the obvious next major step in our voyage of discovery.

By now I was just beginning to acknowledge that I was no longer the same person I had been for the previous sixty-two years. I had learned so much over the past week that I had had some trouble taking it all in. Suddenly there was an acceptance and I felt tremendously happy.

It was wonderful to me to see that, reading between the lines of Fee and Fev's e-mails, we all shared so many of the same values and ideals on which one's life is based. The family and its Christian principles had been the central factors in both of our upbringings. The Bradleys had certainly shared the same values as the Wellingtons. Ma and The Haven had chosen well!

One of the very nicest things about my new-found sisters was the fact that they loved 'finding out'. In this respect they were just like me and as far as the mass of new information was concerned, we were all like sponges and simply soaked up more and more as it became available.

Fee and Fev were obviously reading through everything they had concerning the history of the family, which was an extensive amount. This was another respect in which we were very similar in that I too had inherited all the family papers, certificates and photographs. I have friends here in England who have literally nothing to link them with their family and ancestors. Thank goodness my adoptive parents kept all that 'old family stuff' as I used to call it. The huge box had been in the garage cupboard for years. Only now did it prove so valuable.

From: Fiona
To: Martyn Bradley
Sent: 10 October, 2011
Subject: Another discovery

Dear Ralph,
Oh my goodness I have just made another discovery. This morning I was flipping through the Ralph file, looking at the various documents you have sent us, when I suddenly

noticed something on your baby certificate that I had not seen before.

THE BAPTIST UNION OF GREAT BRITAIN AND IRELAND
(BAPTIST WOMEN'S LEAGUE)

GENERAL SECRETARY:
THE REV. M. E. AUBREY, C.H., M.A.

ORGANISING & DEPUTATION SECRETARY
MISS E. L. CHAPPLE

THE HAVEN
(HOME FOR MOTHERS AND BABIES)

MATRON:
MISS A. K. FINNEY,
S.R.N., S.C.M., M.T.D., D.N. (LOND.)

TEL. YATELEY 3107

VIGO LANE,
YATELEY,
NR. CAMBERLEY

R A L P H.

Date of Birth 8.10.1949.   Birth Weight. 8 lb.7½ ozs.

                               At 25.11.49.   10 lbs.10.ozs.

Feeds: 5 level measures Half-Cream "Cow & Gate"

           5½ ozs. or 11 Tablespoons. hot boiled water.

           (Four-hourly, the last feed 9.30 p.m.)

           Orange Juice - ½ Teaspoon to 1 oz. water.
                (Given by spoon from small cup......4.45 p.m.

           Cod Liver Oil - ¼ Teaspoonful by spoon before 10 a.m.
                and 6 p.m. feeds.

Baby has been successfully vaccinated and circumcised. Sits on

chamber after every feed. Will soon require Full-Cream Cow & Gate.

You know we thought that you were adopted on 19th October, 1949, when you were 11 days old, because that date is on your adoption certificate, and you told us that you thought you had left The Haven on that date. Yet we read in one of the articles that the mothers and babies only left there six weeks after the baby was born. The mothers breastfed for three weeks and then the weaning process began, so that by six weeks everything was back to normal and the babies were on bottles.

R A L P H.

Date of Birth 8.10.1949.   Birth Weight. 8 lb.7½ ozs.

at 25.11.49. 10 lbs.10.ozs.

Well as I said, I was looking at the file this morning and looked at the baby certificate, the one with your birth weight on and what they were feeding you etc. And when I looked closely, I saw 25.11.49, which did not even look like a date to me, but of course it is. It is 25th November 1949. This means that you only left The Haven that day, the day on which you weighed 10 lbs 10 ozs. The baby certificate must be your leaving certificate! It means that you did in fact stay at The Haven with Ma for six full weeks, until the 25th November, **the exact date at which the diary resumes**.

No wonder Ma was rattled on 25th November, the day the diary resumed! No wonder – she had just given away her baby, that very day, and would never see him again. Oh my soul.

You know, I now remember something Ma once told me, around about the time when my babies were little. We were talking about how she had fed Fevvy and me for quite a long time and she went on to say, 'In our day, you know, if you wanted to stop breastfeeding, they used to bind you up with bandages across your chest, to stop you making milk. It was really quite painful.' I had thought it all sounded rather strange and over-dramatic, and hadn't asked too much about it. I didn't ask the obvious question – but Ma, how do you know, since you fed both Fevvy and me for a long time and just weaned us quite naturally? I just let it pass. But now I realise that this is what must have happened to Ma at The Haven when she weaned you on to a bottle at about three weeks old.

Poor Ma. IMAGINE looking after your beautiful little baby for six whole weeks, in fact nearly seven weeks, breastfeeding him and all, and then giving him up and NEVER seeing him again. Oh my soul. How do you live through that?

How indeed.

I had always been puzzled by the two dates on my adoption certificate, the 19th October and then the 18th April 1950. I had assumed that my parents fetched me on the first date, but perhaps it was just the day when they applied to adopt me? Perhaps the second date was the final legal bit? It was rather confusing. Now I realized that this third date, the 25th November, the date on my baby certificate, the date when Ma's diary resumed, was surely the day when I left The Haven, when Ma finally said goodbye to me.

(It was only much later that we worked out, by studying my birth and adoption certificates properly, what had actually happened on 19th October 1949. It was simply the date on which Ma had registered my birth. It says so on both certificates! It had no significance other than that.)

Soon Fee and Fevvy were telling me how they had noticed that in Ma's letter-diary the pages had been freshly numbered in her handwriting with a red felt-tipped pen, the modern pen she had used when she was old and alone. So we knew for sure that she must have re-read that diary and re-lived that momentous time in 1949 when she had me, looked after me and then gave me away.

It comforted me to know that she had thought of me when she was old, but my one great sadness was still that I had never got to meet her. All the more this drove my desire to get to know my sisters more, and for them to know me

So we began to write our life histories for each other, sending instalments via e-mail, illustrated with some rather scary photographs from earlier times. It was uncanny the way in which all these pictures displayed the same family characteristics irrespective of which time period they were from: the squareness of the jaw, the deep-set eyes and most apparent of all, the 'Wellington Nose'. No wonder cousin Arthur had asked if I had any pictures showing profiles when I e-mailed him after Diane had put us in contact!

Ma – 1967; myself and Abi.

Fevvy sent me a 1937 photo of Ma at ten years old. I dug out a photo of Abi at the same age, and couldn't believe how alike the two images were.

Left to right: Abi, 1993; Ma, 1937

I spent some time sorting out CDs to post to Fee and Fevvy, sending them a photo of an old me with my concertina.

A week later, Fevvy wrote: 'Your CD has arrived and I nearly crashed the car going to fetch it at the post office. Just wonderful and we have been listening and listening to it. The sound a concertina makes is just incredibly beautiful and almost haunting – it made me emit some most unladylike sobs!

And as for the photo, it had me gasping... it is just Fee with a moustache!!!'

And then, in an email from Fee:

I had an interesting moment of meltdown yesterday. On a Wednesday as I told you I always go to Klipplaat, a little town half an hour from the farm, and do various things including running an afternoon class for a group of women who are learning to read.

Yesterday's class went just as usual, though I was a little tired. (Surely you're also a bit tired?) I went from table to table giving out worksheets, sitting down at each table in turn to explain to that group of people what they must do on the worksheets, and reading slowly and carefully with them. All as usual. But right at the end of the afternoon I at last gave some attention to the two ladies who are at the 'top' of the class, the two who are able to read the best, who have been learning the longest. They have been working through a series of lessons on the parables of Jesus (they like to read this kind of thing best of all the stuff I prepare for them) and have more or less finished answering all the questions etc., just need to read through the little book of parables a few more times. So I asked them which parable they'd like me to read with them (there are about ten in the booklet). They chose 'Die Verlore Seun' (the direct translation is 'The Lost Son'). I sat down between them as usual and we were reading and reading and all was going fine until we got to the bit that says (in Afrikaans) 'But while he was still a long way off, his father saw him and was filled with compassion for him; he ran to his son, threw his arms around him and kissed him.' To my surprise, I just choked up completely. After clearing my throat a bit and swallowing hard I said to them, 'Oh my goodness I'm not going to be able to read this. Something like this has just happened in our family. Please you two read and I'll just help.' So they read on slowly, aloud, with me prompting them here and there, but by the time they got to killing the fatted calf, tears were just pouring down my face and I was beginning to sob. I escaped and went and hid in the kitchen! That was the end of the lesson, though it took some time for me to recover sufficiently to be able to come out and tell them all that it was time to pack up!

From: Mart Bradley
To: Fee
Sent: 13 October, 2011
Subject: RE: Killing the fatted calf

Hi Fee
What a wonderful story.
Yes, I'm really tired and emotionally drained. I read this and burst into tears – then I had a *really* good cry. After that I felt much better!
Just can't wait to see you. After a 50-year journey I guess a few months is not a long time but it's still going to be a very hard period of time for me.
with love
Ralph

Chapter 22
Meeting my first blood relative

W hile all these emails had been flying back and forth between us, Fee and Fevvy had of course been telling their children about me. Shirley, in London, was the last of them to be told, as she had been away in America visiting her husband's family. Fee sent her this email a few days after we first made contact, though of course I was only shown it much later.

From: Fiona
Sent: 9 October, 2011
To: Shirley Bardone
Subject: Family news

Dear Shirl,
The most startling, amazing, shocking, yet WONDERFUL thing has happened.
You know how when there is a death in the family you are shocked, and spend quite some time unable to come to terms with it, unable to believe it. Well, the *opposite* of a

death has just happened, though the level of unreality and emotion is the same.

Instead of losing someone, we have just, suddenly, and totally unexpectedly, *gained* someone. Fevvy and I are still finding it hard to believe.

Our cousin Arthur phoned me this past Tuesday 4th October and gently told me that someone from England had contacted the Wellington family with momentous news. At first Fevvy and I were very sceptical, but now are convinced of the truth: we have a BROTHER, a half-brother.

We have seen all the birth and adoption certificates, passenger lists, etc., etc. but MOST telling of all are the photos of his family – him, his wife (since 1977) and his daughter. The likeness is unmistakable.

From Wednesday to Friday this past week I was with Fevvy in PE with a violin kid. All the time we were reading through Ma's old letters, diaries and photo albums (thank goodness we had not thrown anything away) – it was like being in a detective story.

We are now convinced that our Ma, your Granny, kept this event a total secret from everyone, even from her own mother, with whom she had a very close relationship and to whom she wrote daily letters in the form of a diary. Yet with the knowledge we now have, the clues are all there. Dad is as amazed and blown away as Fevvy and I are. We spoke to Ralph for the first time today and Dad keeps saying what a lovely person he is. Ralph's daughter, his only child, is called Abigail, a beautiful girl like you and Heather and Laura, about Laura's age we think...

From: Shirley
To: Mart Bradley
Sent: 10 Oct, 2011
Subject: To Uncle Ralph

Uncle Ralph (I hope you don't mind me calling you that!)
I hope you don't mind me emailing you, but I am Fee's
daughter, Shirley, who lives in London. We are absolutely
blown away by the whole story that my mom has relayed
to us via email and over the phone. To say that this has
rocked my mom and Aunty Fev's worlds (well, all of ours,
really!) is something of an understatement, and so very
very exciting! I am still trying to take it all in, but it is
really a miracle that you finally found our family, and it is
so emotional to think about all that Granny Ruth went
through, and how amazing that we have found a new
uncle! We are so blessed. It's almost too much to be able
to process, so incredible.

Anyway, I just wanted to say hi, and how pleased and absolutely thrilled I am. Mom has been absolutely bubbling over every time I hear from her, I don't think she has slept in the last week. It is so special to know that there is another piece of *us* alive in the world, another piece of Granny.

How wonderful and exciting that I have a new uncle! I'm sure you are wonderful, can't wait to meet you!

Take care,

Love Shirley

I wrote back at once:

Hi Shirley

I guess you must be my niece – wow!! How lovely to get your email. I am just totally blown away, along with everyone else I guess – it's been a long, long journey!! I spoke to your mum and to Fev last week and it was just wonderful and somewhat emotional.

Please, please do come down and see us – you will almost certainly be the first real relative that I ever meet!! We are in a little village just outside Chichester in Sussex so it's not a big journey from London – you would all be very, very welcome any time.

Love to you and the family

Uncle Ralph

I got an email from Fevvy's daughter, too:

Dear Uncle Ralph

I thought it would be lovely to email you. Just to say a quick personal hello. Mum and aunty Fee, as you know, are so happy! I'm so excited to know that I have more family to visit in the UK! Mum says that you are all coming over next year March!!! I can't wait... already putting my leave in for work!

Is there any way of contacting my cousin Abigail? Maybe I could email her just to say hi?

Lots of love, Niece Laura

Hi Laura

How lovely to have an email from you.

I'm sure you've seen the pictures of Abi!! I've shown the Christmas picture with you in the blue top to lots of friends here and they all think it *is* Abi. We almost fell off our chairs when we saw it for the first time.

Abi would love to hear from her cousin, she can't wait to see you all.

loads of love, Ralph

So Laura and Abi began a correspondence which would lead them to become close friends, more like sisters than cousins.

Hi Abi

It's me, your 'look alike' cousin! How are you? I can't wait to meet you all! It's so exciting to have more family! I thought I would just email to say hi and tell you a bit about myself...

Dear Laura

I am totally amazed at finding out all about your/our(!) family in South Africa. Dad is simply blown away by it all and we're just so excited about our visit in March next year. It can't come soon enough! I had always wondered if I would even ever see a photograph of Dad's mother; let alone make contact with family...

Not long after this, Helen wrote to her new sisters-in-law.

Dear Fee and Fev,
It must be my turn to say a big hello to you both and all
your families. Your emails with all their photos flying
around the world have been wonderful to behold and
absorb. To suddenly succeed in discovering his real roots
has been a dream come true for Martyn. I must, of course,
get used to also thinking of him as Ralph and shall try and
call him by his true name when talking/writing to
you. Abi too is overjoyed to discover you and all those
cousins and cannot believe all those family likenesses –
not only in looks and mannerisms but, obviously, in
interests and talents as well. The best thing by far is the
fantastic and wholehearted way you have
both/all welcomed us three into your lives and world. So
much still to find out and share but that will continue to
be an exciting journey for a long, long time yet.
Ralph and I met back in 1976 when I sensed he was
someone very special, yet also different from others. That
was all part of his charismatic personality which I fell
for. We married in 1977 and have had a great time
together ever since. Time and again we count ourselves
very lucky. Abi is our greatest blessing as we could not
wish for a more loving and caring daughter who
constantly makes us feel so proud of all her achievements
whilst she somehow retains a very unassuming and
normal outlook on life. Out of her uniform no one would
ever guess she is anything to do with the Army!
Thanks to your many emails I feel I already know quite a
bit about your childhood experiences and busy lives
today. I have many happy memories too and think we
were probably all lucky to grow up in the 50s and 60s

when life was a lot simpler and children really stayed
children for longer. Anyway, I thought you'd like to
know a bit about my early years so I shall endeavour to
give you a potted version...

Helen went on to tell Fee and Fevvy all about her life and her
work as a speech therapist, and they each replied very
enthusiastically. Fevvy wrote: 'So wonderful to hear about you –
we knew Ralph must have married someone special.'

Fee's reply to Helen included this paragraph:

'You mention that you must try to call Martyn by his true
name when talking or writing to us. Please don't worry about that!
He is both Martyn and Ralph to us. He is not more acceptable to
us as Ralph than he is as Martyn. We love both names! I would
hate him to feel that he must downplay the role of his adoptive
parents in any way. They obviously did an awesome job, and I am
sure he was a huge blessing to them, and they to him. I loved
reading of how supportive they were, taking him to gigs etc., as
well as giving him a loving home and happy childhood.'

Fee went on to mention some people she knew who had
adopted a child – how she had seen their anguish at not being able
to have children, their long and desperate waiting for a child to
adopt, and their incredible joy at finally being given a baby to
love. I knew it had been like this for my parents, too.

Thus gradually we all got to know each other by
correspondence. Near the end of November, one of many emails
was this one from Fee:

Dear Ralph,
It may be raining very hard there in England but it is
certainly also raining e-mails on you! We hope you are
surviving the flood!
On top of all the instant mail, I have just posted

something to you – it should get to you in a few weeks. Fevvy and I have now finally decided that you are ready to be subjected to what we call 'The Masterpiece'. Let me explain...

About 30 years ago, when I was first married to Rob and loving living on our farm, I got the urge to write a book about the childhood holidays that Fevvy and I spent visiting our Granny – your Granny, too – at Wilton, the Karoo farm where her brother lived and where she had grown up. I wrote quite a bit in longhand in an exercise book. A few months later, Fevvy came to visit me on our farm and I decided to show her my efforts. I expected her to be very impressed, but instead, she burst out laughing and admitted that she too had started writing about the very same thing! We were amazed that we shared exactly the same urge to write about Wilton, and decided we had better pool our efforts and write the story together. Right from that moment, we referred to it, somewhat sarcastically, as 'The Masterpiece'.

We've been writing it on and off ever since, sending chapters backwards and forwards to each other – by post in pre-e-mail days, of course. In about 1991, we got our Dad to do some sketches for it. Three years ago Rob had a back operation and had a few setbacks while recovering from it. Our son David came to help with the farming, because for about six months Rob mostly had to lie down and I hardly left the house at all. During that time, I began an intensive re-write. E-mails flew back and forth between Fevvy and me as the chapters were revised. It was all great fun, and by about 2009, two years ago, the text was more or less finished. We printed a draft copy, and decided we needed more sketches. Our friend Dawn did some lovely ones for us, and then one day Fevvy decided that she could perhaps try drawing too, though she had never done much before. Well, she sent the sketch to me, and I was gobsmacked! It looked awesome! So for the past year or two Fevvy has been delighting us with her efforts, and 'The Masterpiece' is now full of her drawings. And then YOU found us!! 'The Masterpiece' suffered extreme neglect for a while (it seemed totally tame and pathetic in comparison with what we were experiencing!), but a few weeks ago we realised that it contains quite a lot of family history that you might enjoy. We also realised that we had better finish it off and get it to you before you come out to South Africa, in case you want to visit the places mentioned in it. So I have printed it up for you on our home computer.

So, be warned! Our craziness is on its way to you, for better or worse. We wrote the book for ourselves, to preserve the past, but also for our grandchildren (most as yet unborn), who quite probably will grow up far away and won't know what a Karoo farm is like. And now we discover that we have a BROTHER who has never been to the Karoo, so perhaps unconsciously we wrote it for you too!

No-one knows about this book except us and our poor husbands (who have encouraged us) and the cousins who feature in the book – we ran it past them in 2009. So it is with some trepidation that we're sending it to you – subjecting you to it, as I said – but we feel we must, before you come out here.

About a week later, there was a knock at my door and the thick A4 manuscript arrived. *Two Weeks at Wilton*. There was a card: 'Dear Ralph, Helen and Abi, Happy Christmas! Our first Christmas of knowing you! We hope this home-printed book will give you a taste of Africa and of veld and family, before you get here. With lots of love, Fee and Fev.'

And so I settled down to absorb this detailed account of the family I was born into but had never known. The African childhood I had missed. I enjoyed reading about Ma in the book – they painted her as a loving and competent mother, the source of much sensible advice. My grandmother was there too, at last becoming more than just a name to me.

I particularly liked this passage, which mentioned Ma in England (written with Fevvy as narrator):

The narrow river bed had bare earth banks, dusty and dry. Its floor was loose sand and stones, with no hint of water anywhere. Suddenly I remembered something that Ma had once said to me. When she was young, before she got married, she went and worked in England for a few years. Towards the end of her time there, she found herself becoming very homesick.

'It was so wet and green there in England,' Ma told me, 'so very very green, that I just *longed* to see a dusty, dry, Karoo donga again!'

Now I was walking in a dusty dry river bed myself. Soon it would become a deep donga. I felt quite excited.

Sure enough, it quickly got deeper. Before long the bare earth walls on each side of me were towering above me and I felt as if I was walking in a real canyon. Ma would *love* this, I smiled to myself.

The book made me even more impatient to get to South Africa and connect with my roots. It also inspired me to hurry up and finish the next instalment of my own life story and e-mail it to my sisters.

And then, on 3rd December 2011, the world of writing, of letters and emails, (not to mention the fifty years of research) was at last transposed into physical reality. Getting to know each other remotely became actually meeting a family member face to face for the first time. Shirley would be the first blood-relative I would ever meet – apart from Abi, of course, who was Shirley's cousin, and who shared the Wellington genes and looked so similar.

On the journey up I was deep in thought, very happy thoughts tempered by a slightly humorous feeling of apprehension. I felt rather like the new boy for the first time about to face the headmaster of the school he really wants to join! I knew my sisters would have been in close touch with Shirley and, no doubt, would be eagerly awaiting reports of our visit. I needed to be on my best behaviour!

We had a wonderful time from the moment Shirley opened the front door, although she must have found my staring at her rather disconcerting! In real life she was even more like her cousin Abi than she had been in photos.

Shirley and Simon gave us a really warm welcome and the time just flew. Having seen so many photographs and read so much about them, it was a bit like meeting old friends that we actually had never met. We did not stop talking from the minute we arrived. I kept returning to the one fact that dominated the day for me and made it so different a visit from any other I had ever experienced: here I was in the company of people, lovely people, to whom I was related. We shared both blood and genes and in every way I did finally belong. Yes, the lunch was great, the walk to the park with the children was good fun as was the adventure playground, but the big difference that made every facet of the day wonderful was that this was my family.

The only disappointing aspect of the day was that, due to a previous engagement, Abi could not accompany us. It would have been so good to see the two cousins together for the first time. However, I knew a meet-up would be planned very soon.

Everything about the day reinforced how blessed I felt having discovered such a wonderful family. We shared so many of the same values and ideals. It had been a monumental day for me.

Whilst driving home, I chuckled to myself as I wondered just how long the account of our visit would take to reach South Africa.

Not long at all!

From: Shirley Bardone
To: Rob Hobson
Sent: 3 December, 2011
Subject: Ralph's visit

Hi Mom and Dad

I just wanted to say what a lovely time we had with Helen and Ralph this afternoon. They are very sweet, lovely people, and I especially enjoyed talking to Helen – she was so great with the kids. There's something wonderfully familiar about Ralph – a sort of bumbling comfortableness which I quite liked. Physically he is very like Keith – tall and lean. His eyes reminded me of Granny's, but are a more piercing blue. In personality he is quite strong, personable and has an infectious laugh, but at the same time is gentle and quite humble. What a lovely man.

As I said, I absolutely loved Helen. She and I both felt as though we had known each other for years, and it was fascinating talking to her about her work in speech therapy.

After lunch we took a walk to Chiswick Park, had tea there, played a while at the jungle gym and then came home again. Simon met us at the park, and then we all came home for supper. They left soon after. How lovely. I really just felt like it was all rather uncanny. They are family, through and through.

Lots of love and will try to phone tomorrow!

Shirley

Dear Shirl,

Oh thank you soooo much for this e-mail! As you know, I was DYING to know how the day went... One can't really know people from just e-mails and a few short phone calls. Ralph's accent is so very very different from ours that we can't yet marry the familiarity of the face and writing to the strangeness of the voice! So it is just LOVELY hearing all this from you. Thank you so much for telling us about it – it has made us most MOST happy... But how we wish we could have been there too!

Chapter 23
Countdown

Once the emotional turbulence of the initial discoveries was over, I needed to get things organised for the future. My mind conjured up a picture of my adoptive father, when I was much younger, sitting in his favourite chair and slowly packing and lighting his pipe. I watched him do this on umpteen occasions and very often, once the pipe was lit, he would come out with one of what I called his 'profound statements'. I've mentioned one of these earlier, when the opportunity arose to go to Australia. Another favourite was – 'You know son, there are two types of people in the world: the talkers and the doers. Be assured the talkers are not necessarily those who become the greatest achievers.' He probably used this one when I'd presented him with one of the many great and brilliant ideas I had had during my teens, none of which ever got off the ground. However, it must have filtered through as I can still quote it verbatim.

I was now faced with just one of those situations. Wonderful emails had been flying up and down the planet each bearing new revelations, so much so that I had little time to think of anything else. Fee, Fevvy and I were deep in the discovery process. We were getting to know each other after so many years, which was wonderful, but 'You must come and see us' was for me the one directive that took over everything. Planning for a visit in March became the prime objective. Taking my father's advice, soon I could write:

> Dear Fee and Fevvy – it is soooo exciting – we have
> booked our flights!!!!! We arrive on 2nd March in the
> afternoon and fly out on the afternoon of Sunday 15th
> April – I've attached a pic of the flight details. Abi is over
> the moon – can't wait to meet her cousins and we are all
> just so excited...

And then my sisters sent me what they called the 'Long Letter', which interrupted but ultimately spurred on even more planning. It was the final result of all their research and reflections about Ma. They had managed to put all their thoughts concerning Ma's story down in a single communication – pages and pages long – which both enthralled me and also made me cry.

It also raised the subject I knew would soon take over as the next great unanswered question: Who was my father? This had been touched on by Diane in her memorable first email but I had not really exchanged any serious ideas about this with my sisters. Now they sent me photos from Ma's albums which Ma had labelled 'Luke', and laid out all the evidence that pointed to him most likely being my father. I wrote back:

> Wow, you really are female Poirots!! As you say, there is
> no proof that the 'Luke' in the pictures is him but from
> what we know from Ma's writings and the ages and dates
> I really don't think there is much doubt.
> Do you know, it's strange, almost spooky in a way, but he
> looks exactly how I imagined he would look! I made the
> mistake of opening the pictures before I read the letter

and opened the group picture first – recognised it as
having been taken at Hogsback (I think, those hills in the
background again) and I said to myself 'that's got to be
him!' I found it very emotional looking at this picture –
Ma looking so vibrant and happy and possibly my father
standing there next to her. If I was looking at the picture
of a man who bore no physical resemblance to me
whatsoever I wouldn't find it so disconcerting, however
there are certain features that I really can't ignore – I've
been staring at it for some time!!

The call of Hogsback started with that long letter and never
went away. I was forming a deep suspicion that both Ruth and
'Luke' had been staying there over the New Year period in 1949.
(This was later confirmed.) Surely my very beginnings, my very
roots, were in the Hogsback mountains.

My sisters had written a very moving conclusion to the Long
Letter:

Unless you can find Jennifer Russell, we will probably
never know all the answers. But Fevvy and I are glad that
now we have finally told you all we can. We know that
your father would have been a man of quality, a good and
intelligent man, for Ma to have loved him. The fact that
things went wrong between them can't diminish our joy at
getting to know you at last and finding that you are such a
wonderful person. The brother we never had! Fevvy said
to me the other day – what a wonderful gift Ma has
given us!
It is just wonderful finding out about your life. What has
also been wonderful for us is finding out more about our
family history, and, of course, getting to know Ma herself
better. We feel that we really understand her for the first

time, and as a result we love her even more than before. What an amazing miracle it all seems to be.

So now we have the future to look forward to – getting to know you better, and meeting you, Helen and Abi next year. This past month has truly been the most amazing of our lives.

The Long Letter set me off on a new spurt of family history research, digging into online archives, like census lists, that had recently become available.

On old hand-written records, I saw my grandfather's parents at their address in Cornwall, with my grandfather listed first as a baby in the 1881 census, then as the ten-year-old eldest of a whole family of children in 1891, and then, in the next census ten years later, not there at all. I knew that by 1901 he had already left, as a young probationary minister, to work on the 'mission field' of South Africa.

Dear Fee and Fev,

All this stuff is so fascinating and actually great fun to research. Of course for me it is just so wonderful to *have* a family to research!! Helen and I are really enjoying ourselves and keep going back to look at emails you sent a lot earlier (and of course the Long Letter), to check up on who is who and how they fit into the facts we are discovering.

However, as far as finding Jennifer Russell was concerned, we were not so successful. Helen had suggested we ask our friend Lesley Williams to do the research. Lesley is a keen amateur genealogist and spent much time on the project. After extensive searches throughout all the UK records, censuses and genealogical sites – using Jennifer's exact birth date as known from Ma's diary – she could find nothing we didn't already know. The vision I had had of the sweet old lady recollecting her time spent with Ma and confiding to me the answers to all our questions, is not to be.

To off-set this disappointment, Fee and Fevvy unearthed fascinating information about the Cornish Wellingtons, and even some about the family of 'Luke'.

Fevvy sent me pictures of our grandparents when they were young. This time I could see both myself and Abi there.

Grandmother Muriel; Grandfather Arthur

Fee located someone with a collection of historical Graaff-Reinet newspapers, and spent a day studying and photographing articles in them. Reading these made that period in my grandparents' lives come alive to all of us, and especially to me. Fee sent me church notices, and I saw that my grandfather preached his last sermon in Graaff-Reinet on 17th July 1927. We read a long account of a farewell supper held for the Wellington family just before that. It seemed that the family were well loved by the community, and that my grandfather had had a hand in many projects in the town – for example, in the establishment of the local hospital and school.

The very last thing about the Wellingtons in those newspapers was Ma's birth notice.

She was born at the hospital in Fort Beaufort just 12 days after our grandfather's last Sunday in Graaff-Reinet. How we all wished we could have known more about what it was like for our grandmother to make that big move when so heavily pregnant, and to have her baby born so soon after setting up home in a strange new place.

In other articles dug up by my sisters I read about my grandfather's death at Healdtown in 1944, after he had been governor there for seventeen years. How he died peacefully at home, proclaiming he was 'surrounded by love'. Fee sent me something that Ma had written about how her father, knowing that he was dying, kept saying he felt thrilled to know everything he had ever preached and believed was really true.

How I longed to visit Healdtown and Hogsback and all the places where the family had lived. Our big trip in March 2012 was truly going to be the trip of a lifetime.

I was particularly keen to take some special gift with me for my sisters but the big question naturally was – what? Any final decision was complicated by the fact that there were two of them – this was wonderful of course but made choice rather difficult. I could not take separate presents for the two of them – it had to be something that would be exactly the same for both of them – and I didn't want to take something they would have to share. No, that wouldn't do at all. I finally had inspiration from a good friend whose father-in-law had an important birthday coming up. She told me she was secretly producing a photo-book with an online company, using lots of old family photographs, which would be presented to him at the birthday party.

My Secret Project was a true labour of love, although I did not realise when I started that it would take up over 120 hours. Here was the perfect opportunity to use photos to tell the story of my life up to now that my sisters had never known. The 'old family stuff' in the garage was upgraded to the study and the delving began.

Once I had decided on the format of the Secret Project, it quickly became the most important aspect of the preparations for the big voyage of discovery. I thanked my adoptive mum once again for keeping so many of the old family photographs. These were in several old sweet boxes as well as a set from my first year of life which were actually in an album. By the time the section of the project that covered my early childhood was complete, I had used over fifty pictures. These had all been resized, located within the page designs and then commented on. There was still a long way to go!

My sisters often referred to it with growing curiosity: 'We are so glad that the agony of being agog for so long in wondering about the *Secret Project* is nearly over – heh heh it's been such fun speculating as to what it might be...'

As the day of departure loomed closer, the level of excitement rose rapidly, as did the expectation. The plans which Fee and Fevvy had come up with for the seven-week visit were just brilliant and, as well as time spent at their respective homes in Port Elizabeth and on the farm near Graaff-Reinet, included time at Hogsback and Healdtown and at a big family wedding in Cape Town. Abi's cousin – Fee's daughter, Heather – was getting married and we would be there. The whole trip was developing an unreal dreamlike quality about it and I went back to pinching myself!

Fevvy wrote:

Dennis (my school principal) is having a fit because I will be gone for so long but he agrees that I have to take time off. He refers to your imminent arrival as 'The Big Hollywood Moment'. When I first told him about you last October, he was just totally blown away by your story. He just kept saying – 'it's just like a film – can't believe it'... but then of course, he *did* have to say at the end... 'But who would want to spend 50 years looking for *you*...'!

In the last week before our trip, Fevvy heard from an old friend. About ten years before, Leonie had lived with Fevvy's family for several months, and had got to know Ma really well.

Leonie had since moved overseas and they had lost contact. Now Fevvy filled her in on what she called 'the Ralph story'. Leonie's responses are worth sharing here:

Nooooo waaaaaaaayyyy!!!! How wonderful!!! I've smiled and brimmed up with tears reading your story. And the photos! I would have sworn that Abi was Laura... What a journey and it's only the beginning.

Amazing. My heart bleeds for your mom – how tragic it must have been for her to let him go.

I think for an adopted child, finding roots is a such a much HUGER thing than we can ever imagine. Four years ago when my husband's sister met her grown-up daughter for the first time, it was evident. The daughter looked at her mother's feet and realised that they looked like hers and she said, 'Now I feel like I belong', despite the fact that she's been raised in a very loving home. That made me cry!!!

It's amazing closure. I can't imagine how searching for 50 years must make one feel – thank God it was worth it... wow, what determination.

Enjoy the Big Hollywood Moment... it's a reminder of how it'll be in heaven... imagine all the reunions!

The final week before we embarked on our big trip seemed to last an eternity and, although there was much to do before we left for the airport, I found it hard to concentrate and was sure I would forget something crucial. I imagined suddenly waking up on the plane to discover I had left the Secret Project behind. On another occasion I woke from a dream where we were on a plane to the Belgian Congo which had been turned back to London because I had forgotten to bring my luggage! How swiftly dreams become those strange visions.

Just before we left, I sent an explanatory email to all my friends around the globe:

From: Mart Bradley/Ralph Wellington

Hi All

As most of you know, we are off to South Africa on Thursday for the sort of journey that comes once-in-a-lifetime and, only then, if you're really lucky – I'm feeling very blessed at the moment!!

The last four and a bit months since discovering my real family has been the most wonderful and emotional period of my life and the story reaches its peak on Friday when I finally meet up in Port Elizabeth with my two incredible sisters, Fiona and Heather, and their families. All the members of the extended Wellington family have been just so welcoming and wonderful since October 4th, and the next seven weeks, during which we will meet them all, are going to be something of an emotional rollercoaster!!

The huge flurry of replies wishing us well that came in during the following day or two was quite overwhelming. I was indeed feeling very blessed and even quite humble.

Meanwhile, in South Africa, preparations were also being made:

Fiona:

When there was only a week or so to go, I had a phone call from my sister-in-law Karen, who is married to Rob's brother Harold. (All of Rob's family had been thrilled to learn about our brand new brother, and had read some of the early e-mails that had passed between us.) Karen and I chatted about Ralph, Helen and Abi's upcoming visit and how we were all looking forward to it. Rob's family – his parents and brothers and sisters – would all get to meet Ralph at my daughter Heather's wedding, which would take place in Cape Town in March. Everyone would be there, family old and new, and it was going to be a great occasion.

Karen and I chatted happily, and then she began to sound a little awkward.

'Sandy and I were talking on the phone the other day,' she began. (Sandy is Rob's sister.) 'We had an idea, well, it was Sandy's idea. But we don't want to interfere.'

'How do you mean, interfere?' I asked gently.

'Well, we had a suggestion to make, you know, about when your brother comes, but, well, we don't, as I've said, we don't want to interfere or anything.'

'Oh, I won't mind,' I said. However she persisted in being reluctant to tell me their idea, saying again that they didn't want to presume to make suggestions, etc., until at last I persuaded her, urging her, 'Please, please, just tell me.'

And so she told me. Oh my.

Wow. Of course. How wonderful. Why didn't we think of that ourselves?

I swallowed hard, and managed to whisper into the phone, 'thank you'. I wasn't able to say anything more, and had to hang up without saying good-bye. But Karen understood.

Heather:

When Fee phoned and told me what Karen and Sandy had suggested I thought it a brilliant idea. We would have our own 'Secret Project' but, of course, we wouldn't mention a word about it to Ralph. I did tell Adrian though and after giving his nose a good blow, he agreed it was a wonderful plan.

I set out the very next day to organise what we wanted to do.

When the saleslady in the shop, a lovely woman of about my age, enquired as to why I needed something particular done, I started telling her the 'Ralph Story'. Her eyes got bigger and bigger and in no time, there were tears trickling down her face (as well as mine) and she begged me to bring Ralph into the shop when they all came out. I shared my tissues with her and promised to bring him with me to meet her in just over a week, when we would all be together.

I went home feeling excited and grateful that Karen had phoned Fee and couldn't wait to let Fee know that our Secret Project would soon be ready for collection.

From: Abi Bradley
To: Fiona; Heather
Sent: 1 March, 2012
Subject: Hello from Abi!

To my lovely aunts...
I actually can't believe this is happening. There is what I would call an 'admin explosion' in the hallway; our bags all half-packed and various clothes in the final stages of drying after Mum's extensive washing frenzy over the last couple of days. We're almost ready. I think that when the taxi calls tomorrow afternoon the adrenaline will kick in and I will realise this is, indeed, real.
Dad is quite obviously so excited he can't think straight and I doubt he'll sleep tonight. It is like a child at Christmas who actually knows he is going to come face to face with THE real Father Christmas!
It's been great to swap e-mails with Laura over the past weeks and I am so looking forward to meeting her and my many other cousins. It really will feel the closest I have had to having siblings – still can't get over the family

resemblance. I'm sure I'll have to stop myself from staring and staring at you all and working out who I must look like!

We'll be winging our way to you this time in 24hrs time – simply amazing. See you in PE!!

Lots of love,

Abi xxxx

From: Fiona
To: Heather
Sent: 2 March, 2012 5:49 AM
Subject: It's today!

Dear Fevvvrrr

Hellooooo! Didn't sleep all that much, wonder about you? My goodness, it's **THE day**!!!

Chapter 24
Together at last

The journey, when 1st March finally arrived, was just as exciting as any travelling could be. The time spent waiting around at airports, checking in, clearing security and walking what seems miles and miles to distant check-in gates is usually extremely tedious. Not on this occasion. Flight SA237 took off from Heathrow on time, just after nine in the evening, and we were on our way.

My new Wellington cousins in Johannesburg had arranged to meet us at the airport once we had cleared South African immigration. We had an hour or so free before we needed to check-in for the flight down to Port Elizabeth and there was to be a family welcome awaiting us. I usually sleep very well on long-haul flights but this time it was hours before I even came close to drifting off. There was far too much whizzing round my brain and vying for my attention simultaneously but always ending with visions of the same moment – the meeting in Port Elizabeth. I imagined it so many times throughout the long night, finally getting a nap in the early hours.

It was almost exactly twelve hours after leaving Heathrow that we landed at O.R. Tambo in Johannesburg and cleared the long immigration lines. I'm not normally very awake at this early hour but on this occasion all three of us were bright-eyed and full of anticipation.

As we at last cleared customs and rounded the final corner, there at the front of the arrivals lounge was our wonderful welcome. Cousin Wendy, sister of Arthur in Cape Town, and her husband, known as Sparky, were there together with Penny (widow of cousin Doug, Diane's brother) from Pretoria and her son Lloyd. Once we had found a table and some coffee we started talking and never stopped until we were running out of time and had to hot-foot it to the domestic terminal.

Penny had produced a wonderful photo album for me of the Pretoria side of the family, spanning the years from the 50s to the present. She wrote in the front:

Dear Ralph, Helen and Abi,

Welcome to the family; welcome to South Africa!

I have put together some photos. I hope they will help you to know something about your family of cousins from Pretoria.

With lots of love and many blessings, from Penny Wellington.

I was overwhelmed with joy and only just managed to contain the emotions as I read these lines over and again awaiting the flight to Port Elizabeth, the very last leg of an incredibly long journey!

I wondered how my sisters were feeling.

Heather

To say I was nervous would be silly. I felt totally terrified when I awoke on Friday, 2nd March. In fact, terrified and also terribly excited explains it exactly. How does one meet one's brother for the first time when one is 56 years old? I felt I knew him quite well from all the emails and phone calls – the phone calls were hilarious, of course – a very foreign accent speaking to me and my mind telling me that this is Ma's son, my brother – but... 'What if they don't like us?' I felt sick in my tummy. After nearly six months my mind had still not adjusted to this incredible happening... and today was D-Day. I hid under my duvet a bit longer.

I was going to go to school, as normal, as I knew it would help to calm me, and then would leave at noon to meet up with Fee and Rob at our house before setting off to the airport. But goodness me, the day had finally arrived and I was plain terrified.

I had had great fun in the days before today, buying little South African gifts to welcome them all here. They would each get a carved wooden bowl filled with sweets, Amarula Cream liqueur, beaded giraffes, mosquito repellents, PE bookmarks – all sorts of goodies. I checked on them, all wrapped and ready on Ralph and Helen's bed, one more time before I left for school.

What had been most exciting though was having photographs of Ralph, Helen and Abi printed and framed, together with pictures of Ma (one taken in May 1949 when she must have been pregnant with Ralph) and hanging them in the passage outside their bedroom. I was like an excited child getting ready for Christmas.

I remember looking at the clock in my office at school just about every ten minutes. My wonderful principal Dennis had readily agreed to give me nearly a month's leave from school – well, one week would be in the holidays anyway. Our conversation about my need for leave still makes me chuckle when I think of it: I had said to him just after Christmas that I wanted to have a meeting before the new school year started. This seemed to alarm him tremendously. When I got there he hurried me through to his office, urged me to sit down and asked me what

I needed to see him about. I reminded him about Ralph and said that what I needed was just a few weeks of leave. He sighed and smiled. 'Oh of course, is that all? I was worried you were going to resign!'

I found it impossible to concentrate on any real bursar work – my head was so full of what was about to happen. I smiled as I let my mind go over all we had planned.

There was to be a special 'Welcome to Africa' braai on their second night with us and I wanted to make something different, something African, for the evening. Some weeks before, I had driven past my old house where my kids had grown up and where I had lived with Gavin, and had stopped to admire the coral tree on the pavement outside the house. I had planted this tree myself many years ago. It was particularly special to me as it had been grown from a seed of the tree in Ma's garden, which in turn she had grown from a seed of the tree in her grandmother's garden in Somerset East.

Somehow the 'family tree' seed thing had made me think. I loved the coral tree seeds, beautiful vivid orange 'lucky beans' – the exact same bright orange as the aloe flowers on Fee's farm. I could use them to decorate serviette rings for the special night.

Dawn and Laura came round often to help and we had spent many happy hours sitting in our courtyard, sipping coffee or wine, talking non-stop and making the little napkin rings. Adrian had cut some strong cardboard tubing for me to the right width and we had glued the bright orange seeds closely together all over the outside of the rings. Once varnished, the flame-coloured little beans almost seemed to glow. We were most happy with our efforts and thought they would give a definite 'family' African tone to the long table when it was set for the planned supper in the courtyard.

All was ready I reassured myself yet again as I looked at the school clock for the hundredth time that morning – goodness, it was time to leave. Quickly I packed up my office and hugged our principal and secretaries goodbye in the foyer before hurrying out of the school building. Oh dear, I was so terrified... once home, time would rush by and we would soon be on our way to the airport!

Fee and Rob were there when I got home and so was Dawn – she and Adrian would take photos. 'Take hundreds,' I told them for the umpteenth time... I felt better – well, slightly calmer. Fee was here and we would meet Ralph together.

At the airport, we sat at a big window in the restaurant upstairs and stared out at the long runway as we waited for Ralph's plane to arrive. For the very first time in my life, I was worried I was about to have a heart attack. I needed to calm down but nothing helped.

A plane landed... but it was not yet *the* plane. We waited some more until a plane landed that we knew just had to be bringing Ralph – we listened to the announcement – and it was. Gulp!

Fiona

I wasn't nervous or scared, just very excited. I knew that we would all get on well – the five months of e-mails that we had exchanged had made me sure of that. The Port Elizabeth airport is so small you can see each plane arrive and can watch it coming closer, knowing exactly which aircraft it is and when it is Your Plane, the One you are waiting for. No plane has ever been more keenly anticipated than the one which arrived at midday that day, 2nd March 2012. And I know that Ralph felt the same, because just as we were taking countless photos of his plane arriving, so he was taking photos through the cabin window of the airport getting closer.

I don't remember anything at all about that short flight. I'm sure we talked about how great the time in Johannesburg had been and I'm even more sure we talked about what was to come so very soon. I'm certain I didn't sleep at all as I was far too excited, but I remember nothing at all until I saw the sea from my window seat and realised how little time there was to go.

One thing that struck me at the time was just how bright the colours were. Rather like my first impression of Australia many years before. After a very long banking turn out over the sea, we lined up for the final approach and landed at Port Elizabeth. As we taxied up to the terminal I was glued to my window, scanning the windows of the arrivals building, but could see nothing within.

Everything from that point onwards seemed to be so very slow. The stop, gathering the bags from the overhead lockers, waiting for the doors to open and for people to start moving. We were right at the back so were almost last off the plane.

The walk down the steps and across the tarmac was intense and I think my heartbeat set new levels of attainment until we entered arrivals and there, across the hall, beyond the luggage-claim, right by the entrance to the terminal, were Fiona and Heather waving madly.

Luggage completely forgotten, I walked straight out through the entrance into the arms of my sisters. This time the emotions were not contained at all! I did not want to let Fee and Fevvy go and held the both of them on and on. I clearly remember thinking at the time: 'Ma, are you seeing this?!' I cried, I think we all cried, but the tears were tears of the utmost happiness.

At last, after all the years apart we were together, we were a family.

I'm not sure how long the meeting-up actually took, probably no longer than five or ten minutes, but these were the most wonderful minutes of my entire life. The whole episode was photographed by my extremely patient new brothers-in-law, Rob and Adrian, and Fevvy's close friend, Dawn. She had been in the car with Fevvy when Fee first phoned with the news of my existence so she knew exactly what this meant to all of us.

It was, of course, just wonderful to meet up with her, and with Rob and Adrian. Both men were tall and grey-haired, smiling and, I thought, must be extremely accommodating! They had suffered the endless, emotional email trail right from cousin Arthur's phone call and were here now happily snapping away in the background. I knew from the start that as well as being relations, they were destined to become firm friends.

Heather

Standing downstairs waiting to see the real live Ralph seemed to take forever. Now I thought a heart attack was really and truly on the cards. I was sure the others could hear the thudding inside my chest.

We had never Skyped him... we felt we had to meet him face to face and in the flesh for the very first time, as it was far too huge an event to try to handle using something as impersonal – we needed to be able to hug him.

Passengers appeared to be in no hurry at all and we could see groups of people chatting to each other and walking annoyingly slowly along towards the airport building. We waited and waited.

Then at last we saw Ralph. He wasn't ambling and talking like the other passengers. He came striding along, passing other passengers, and into the arrivals hall – and then we could see Helen and Abi following closely behind him.

Ralph didn't wait to collect his luggage, he just kept on striding – he had spotted us, and came straight through the big glass doors and into our arms.

Fee and I held him so tightly we could hardly breathe, while tears ran down our cheeks. We were holding our brother for the very first time – 'Oh Ma, can you see us?' flashed through my mind. (We later found we had all thought that.)

What must all the people around us be thinking – all the photos being taken and us looking so tearfully happy? I quickly tried to pull myself together before hugging Abi and Helen. It was a strange feeling meeting your blood brother for the first time. You recognised him as your family – yet he was unknown. It was far stranger than just looking at a photograph and recognising your family likeness – this was him in the flesh.

Abi in real life was even more like one of our own children than the photos had shown – oh it was amazing, and of course, lovely Helen, we knew, would be a wonderful new sister for us as well. It was just so much to take in.

We were all together at last.

Fiona

We left the airport, and everything felt new to me. I seemed to be seeing Port Elizabeth as if for the first time. I had felt like this only once before – after our first baby was born and we were leaving the hospital to go home: after such a momentous event I had felt that the whole world looked new, as if it was a completely different place. Now even more so, as we showed our brother our world for the first time. The streets, the houses, the trees, the sky: I felt as if I was seeing everything with new eyes. Ralph said nice things about it all, saying it reminded him of his happy year teaching in Australia. He said that the architecture (for which we were apologising) and the tall gum trees everywhere, which he called eucalypts, made him feel as if he could be right back down under again. He sounded to me a bit like Ma, not with his accent, but with his enthusiasm.

And I was right about us getting on well. Right from the moment we hugged at the airport, we were happy. Usually I feel embarrassed when a camera appears, and struggle to smile naturally, generally looking rather awkward in photos. But not then. For the first time in my life, from that amazing day when Ralph, Helen and Abi's plane touched down and for the whole six wonderful weeks of their visit, I just had a great big happy grin on my face in every picture. We all did.

We were soon at Fevvy and Adrian's house but I'm not too sure how we got there. The meeting itself is such a strong memory that everything around it has paled into insignificance. I do, however, remember thinking that both the houses and the trees in Port Elizabeth reminded me somewhat of Australia. Eucalyptus trees were everywhere, which I found quite surprising. Many of the houses were a mixture of modern designs but there were also examples of much earlier styles with verandahs, the older ones having the ornamental iron lattice work which I had only seen previously in New South Wales. There was also much evidence of Dutch influence with the houses having their typical curved gable ends. It was certainly very different to England!

And then, quite quickly, we arrived at Fevvy's house. A large modern bungalow, it was set in a lovely, leafy suburb, with majestic, mature trees lining the roads. I remember especially the beautiful flowers on the huge pink Hibiscus growing in the front garden, and lamenting that we can't grow them successfully in the UK.

Once we had arrived and carried our luggage inside, Fevvy took us down a long carpeted passage to our room. I suddenly stopped dead and simply stared open-mouthed. We three had travelled for the best part of a whole day to the other end of the world and there amongst the framed family pictures on the wall were pictures of us. I cried yet again.

The first evening together just seemed to develop naturally though I'm sure this was down to some very clever and careful planning and preparation by Fee and Fevvy. We had been given some time to recover from the journey, shower, and generally make ourselves human again and then we all met up for a very welcome drink in the thatched 'braai' (barbecue) area outside of the house by the swimming pool. It was so interesting discovering all the differences between the house here and our house at home. Mind you, I have to say that in the light of the events of the afternoon, everything had changed and all things were very different.

Heather

In no time at all we were sitting outside beneath the thatched braai area waiting for Laura to arrive. I was grateful that even the weather had behaved perfectly and it was the most beautiful, warm and still afternoon.

I felt excited when the doorbell rang and remember hurrying through the house to let Laura in and taking her to meet Abi – and of course, Ralph and Helen – but I wanted to see the two 'lookalike' cousins meeting up for the first time. They hugged and laughed together and then of course, had to pose as we all took photos – they were very tolerant and stood side by side facing us and then even obliged by turning sideways to show off their similar 'Wellington' noses as we clicked away with our cameras. Oh it was wonderful and I don't think any of us stopped smiling and exclaiming that whole amazing afternoon and evening.

Soon Adrian was offering drinks all round and I must admit, the idea of a lovely cold glass of wine to calm the butterflies sounded a brilliant idea.

It was just wonderful seeing Abi and Laura meeting and hitting it off as if they had been friends for years. They had, of course, been relations for years, they just hadn't known it! Abi was to stay with Laura for the duration of the visit, which was just perfect.

Later that afternoon, Fee's son David arrived – a very friendly young man so tall that he had to duck through every doorway. Exactly Abi's age, he looked remarkably like a handsome male version of her. It was amazing for me, who had never known any blood relatives except for Abi, to see so many lookalikes all together. When I commented on David's height, Fee mentioned that there were several tall people in the family, adding, 'And Ma herself was five foot ten, of course.' We had always wondered where Abi got her height!

My sisters had promised that the next day, when we had all recovered a little, they would show me everything they had found out about Ma and the past. I couldn't wait to see Ma's diary – I wanted to read every word as I knew that not only would I be able to get to know Ma through Fee and Fevvy but also by reading what she herself had written. There were all Ma's photo albums to go through, as well as grandmother's little address book and Ma's 1948 passport (which Fee and Fevvy insisted that I keep and which is now one of my most treasured possessions). But now, our very first afternoon, was a time for just enjoying being together.

It was difficult to take in my new surroundings as I spent most of the time staring at all these people who looked like me. When the warm African afternoon became evening, Fevvy appeared with a can of the essential mosquito repellent. I was wearing my summer sandals, and, still holding my beer, obediently stretched out a foot to be sprayed. Fevvy stopped dead, and exclaimed in amazement, 'Goodness! You have my feet!' She stood next to me and held her foot next to mine. The shape and length of each toe, the look of the whole foot – identical. A great comparing of feet then happened, to everyone's amusement. We laughed a lot at what Fevvy called our beautiful twin feet!

The wonder of it all just never stopped amazing me. That first day together was probably the best day of my entire life.

Chapter 25
The secret projects

As we sat there in the garden relaxing with my family, it became clear to me that this was the ideal moment for presents. Fevvy had left a wonderful 'Welcome to Africa' collection on our bed which we planned to open later, and Helen had given my sisters each a pretty apron, but now was the time for something special from me. I went to our room, opened my suitcase and unpacked two identical parcels – my Secret Project.

Fiona:

I leant back on my seat, sipping my Coke, feeling happy and contented. Then Ralph put his beer down, gave us sisters a huge mischievous grin, wagged his finger at us and said, 'Ah hah... the Secret Project!'

He disappeared into the house. I looked at Fevvy sitting next to me and could see her eyes getting big. She looked at me and I knew she too was feeling excited and bursting with curiosity – what could it be? We had wondered and speculated for so many months.

They made sure they opened their gifts at exactly the same time and speed and there they were, two identical copies of 'Ralph Allan Wellington – My Life in Pictures'. Although it was a book about me, I had started the first page with the picture of Ma on the *Capetown Castle* during her voyage to England in 1949. I could tell by the look on both my sisters' faces that the Lady of Shalott was weaving her magic yet again.

Fiona

Ralph soon reappeared holding what looked like two thin, flat, grey boxes – each was a cardboard sleeve protecting a book inside. Carefully we tipped them out. On the front of each was a picture of Ralph as a baby, and with many joyful exclamations we realised that Ralph's long-awaited Secret Project was a photobook filling us in on the sixty-two years of his life that we had missed. What

a wonderful gift. And no wonder it had taken him so long to make!

From his e-mails we knew about his childhood, his teaching, and his involvement in the folk music scene in England, but here were many interesting things we knew nothing about at all. Totally fascinating. We sat riveted, paging through.

Heather

The book started with The Haven... and then baby pictures of Ralph. Under them, he had written:

'My adoptive parents, Dorothy and Dick Bradley, christened me Martyn Richard Bradley. They were very proud and showed me off to all the relations.'

Then there were photos of Ralph with a toy train and beneath them was the caption:

'This was my 2nd birthday on 8 October 1951, and here I am proudly showing off my favourite present from Mum and Dad. I had a wonderful, happy childhood, with lots to do and good friends to do it all with.'

We looked through the whole book, though far too quickly in our excitement, seeing some pictures which had been sent to us in e-mails – like the one of Ralph and Helen's wedding, which I had put into the big frame outside their bedroom here – and many which we had never seen at all. I needed time to sit by myself and read it all properly but I could see that Fee was already a few pages ahead of me and so turned to the last page of the book. I gulped when I saw a picture of us two sisters (the one we had sent him with our first email) and then read what Ralph had written.

'It might seem that the previous page clearly marks the end of this book but that is not the case. Just occasionally things happen which have a profound effect on life itself. The reason this book exists at all is due to one such event. Just a few months ago, on 4 October, and after years of trying, I discovered the true story of Ruth Wellington, my mother, and my real family. These last months have been the most exciting and emotional period of my life. For the first time I know who I really am, where I come from and who those closest to me are. So, this book is not the end of the story but is very much the beginning of the next part of the story.'

Goodness, my emotions were in overload and the tears were starting again. This was the beginning of a new story *for us all*.

I knew I would need to sit quietly by myself and read and absorb every word of the book, but now I looked over at Fee to see if she was thinking what I was thinking... she gently nodded her head and smiled, so I knew she was.

It was now my turn to disappear into the house, with a 'We've got something for you too, Ralph.' Goodness, I could feel my heart pounding as I got the present out of my cupboard.

Fee stood up when I came outside again as we wanted to give him our gift together. So with our lovely husbands, and Helen and Abi, Laura, David and Dawn all watching, we gave him our wrapped-up package – just a little square box.

The evening passed quite slowly and I simply remember it as being perfect. I kept pinching myself thinking I was going to wake up and discover it was all a dream.

I'm not sure how long it took Fee and Fevvy to complete looking through the book but it was an immensely enjoyable time, talking to Rob and Adrian while the exclamations continued as my sisters discovered and read about yet another photograph from my past. I don't think I even realised they had finished when Fevvy said, 'We've got something for you too, Ralph.'

She held out a small parcel for me to open. Fee stood up and they gave it to me together. 'This is from us with love,' is all they said. I couldn't read their expressions exactly but I could tell from their smiles that this was going to be something very special.

As I unwrapped the small square parcel, I had no idea at all what it might be. It did not take me long to open it, and there it was. My mind whirred back to a dim and distant time, fifty years ago.

There, nestling in the jeweller's packaging, lay a gold watch. The gold watch, not given to me that Christmas when I was twelve because I wasn't blood family – I didn't belong. And here it was.

I lifted it out and turned it over. There was an inscription: '4th OCT 2011 LOVE YOUR SISTERS'. My inscribed gold watch.

After fifty years of searching and heartache and then, at last, discovery, I was family and I finally did belong. I couldn't say a word. The silent hug I gave Fee and Fevvy spoke for itself.

Epilogue – South Africa, 2019

So there we have it. What started so long ago with one old man's rejection of his great grandson has come full-circle. The lack of one gold watch has led through years studded with both heartbreak and elation, to the possession of another... one of so much greater value. The story of my search is complete but this cannot be the ending, however convenient it may seem to be.

I am writing this on the stoep of Fee and Rob's farmhouse, overlooking the vast landscape of the Karoo, a wild place; hot and dusty, and so very different from where I live in England. Yet I feel at home here. I have come to love this place so very deeply. As I look out over the rocky landscape with its hills scarred with ravines and punctuated by windswept trees and the majestic aloes, I find myself relaxing fully.

That first evening together in Port Elizabeth is now more than seven years ago and so much has happened since that memorable occasion. It was evident very soon after that, that a book had to be written, evident because just about everyone who heard the story, told us as much. The book is now finished but I continue to write, inspired by those few who have read the completed manuscript as it stands. They have unanimously returned the same response:

'You can't leave it there! We must know what has happened to you all since then.' So I write the final chapter, the epilogue.

The first thing I want to tell happened a few years after our initial meeting. Fee wrote to me – it had suddenly occurred to her that she should visit Ma's old doctor, and ask him about me. Had Ma perhaps confided in him? Was there someone, after all, to whom she had told her secret? Fee told me all about it in an email:

> He is a man of about our age, who was really good to Ma and Dad in their old age, popping in to see them in their little retirement cottage quite often, unasked, in the evening on his way home after doing his rounds at the hospital nearby. I knew him well, had been to him myself, but somehow Fevvy and I did not think to ask him about Ma's secret when we first heard about you. But last week while in Port Elizabeth I needed to see a doctor as I had nearly lost my voice, and in wondering who to consult, I remembered Ma's doctor. And it just hit me – I should ask him about you! Don't know why we didn't think of this before.
>
> It was lovely to see him again. A great guy. After he had sorted out my sore throat, we chatted about the past. I thanked him for being so kind to my parents during their last years when they were old and ill.
>
> 'Tell me,' I then asked. 'Did my mother... in that sad time after my Dad had died and she was alone... did my mother ever tell you a secret?'
>
> He looked at me without answering. Then he seemed to make up his mind. Smiling, he admitted cautiously, 'Yes.'
> I did not want to hear some other secret that was no business of mine, and did not want to put him in the awkward position of having to betray doctor–patient confidentiality, so I said, 'My sister and I have recently

discovered that we have a brother! Was my mother's secret about a child she had given up for adoption when she was young?'

He smiled more broadly, leant back in his chair, and nodded, 'Yes.'

Oh wow. You can imagine. I said to him, 'Wow, you are the only person, the only living person that we know of, that she ever told. Please, what can you remember? What did she say?'

He said that he really couldn't remember much. 'I think it happened over in England?' he queried.

'Yes,' I said, 'but surely you can remember more? What did she say to you? How did she feel?'

He told me she'd said she had to keep it a secret, but that she wanted to tell someone. I said, 'You mean, she wanted to tell someone before she died?' And he nodded, 'Yes.'

'And she told you because she trusted you.'

He smiled. 'I had a really good rapport with your mother.' I felt quite breathless – as he talked it felt to me like Ma was speaking to me, like at last I was hearing about you in her own words. In the short time available I told him all I could and asked him all I could. He repeated that he couldn't really remember much, as it was so long ago, and also that after she died, he had tried to forget it so as not to betray her confidence. But he recalled that she had said she was very sad that she had never been able to tell Phil (our Dad). And that she was glad to at last be able to tell someone – him, the doctor – about it. I told him how we knew she must have thought a lot about her lost baby during that last year of her life because of the red marks in her diary of 1949, that year when it all happened, in a modern felt-tipped pen, the one she used then. I told him that we now realise that although she was sad that year

(2002–2003) because our Dad had died and she was so ill, she was also sad because of the son that she had had to give away. And he confirmed this. He said she wished she could contact him to find out about his life, but didn't know how, and anyway she couldn't, because it all had to remain a secret.

And that is all. But wow, I left his rooms reeling, feeling that for the first time we were hearing Ma's actual words about you, Ralph. Oh my goodness. At last we know something of what she felt in those sad lonely months before she died.

So. At last I knew. Ma had struggled with her secret knowledge of my existence right until the end. What anguish it must have caused her. My sisters and I have talked many times about the timing of my finding of the family. How for many reasons, it was probably about perfect but I still wonder 'what if'... What if I had found Ma a little earlier, during that last year of her life? Would it not have spared that wonderful lady some of her pain and brought joy to her final year? I still lose sleep trying to answer this.

Our first six weeks together during March and April of 2012 were, for all three of us, the great age of discovery, and it was discovery on two fronts. Firstly, we were experiencing the supreme enjoyment of discovering each other and the myriad 'little things' which made us so obviously siblings. Mannerisms, specific ways of doing things and even the smallest idiosyncrasies were often so very similar. I remember very early on after that initial meeting, Fee and Fevvy commenting on the way I moved my food neatly around the plate at mealtimes in just exactly the same way as Ma had done throughout her life. How could the influence be so apparent from the mother I never met? My sisters have commented on a host of things which I do quite naturally as being 'just so like Ma!' It continues to this day. Sure we had discovered from our early emailing days that we shared many of the same values, but throughout the years since we met, it has gone a lot deeper than that. We share so many interests and our general zest for life is uncannily similar. Not a year has gone by without at least one visit to South Africa and both Fee and Fevvy have reciprocated with visits to the UK, the most memorable being in 2014 when Fee, Fevvy, Rob, Adrian and Laura came over for Abi's wedding to Markis. How wonderful for Abi to have the 'lookalike' cousin as her bridesmaid.

I have changed since becoming a Wellington, for the better I am sure. On their visits to us, Fee and Fevvy have met some of my long-time, close friends, who have commented independently to them that I now have a calmness that was not present previously. The restlessness has gone. I too feel this and put it down to a final sense of belonging, missing in my life for so many years.

The second area of discovery for all three of us has been the family itself. It was apparent very quickly from our months of emailing, both before and after we met, that we shared a great interest in family history. It was a fascinating study, starting with our roots in Cornwall and going back to the settlers of 1820 and the origins of the family in South Africa. All of it held interest but most interesting of all was that relating to our grandfather, Abraham Arthur Wellington. Once we were together it was this area which was to dominate our research and in 2012 we looked forward eagerly to the planned visits to both Healdtown and Hogsback. We were to spend a whole six weeks together, but visiting these two locations was of paramount importance to all three of us.

Looking back now, I can't help being slightly amused by the fact that Hogsback and Healdtown were last on the list. Either by design or fate, they came after we had visited all the other locations which were, and still remain, of central importance to the family's life in South Africa: the farm near Somerset East where my grandmother had grown up, and which I had read about in Fee and Fevvy's 'masterpiece'; the little church at nearby Middleton where my grandparents married; and the manse in Graaff-Reinet where the family lived before moving to Healdtown, just before Ma was born.

At the start of this, our first epic visit, we spent time at Fevvy and Adrian's house in Port Elizabeth and then travelled 200km north west to Fee's farm in the Karoo. The Swart River farmhouse is beautiful, built of stone with a huge stoep on which to relax, surrounded by enormous green trees including some eucalypts – the scene reminded us so much of the farms we saw in Australia in 1991. I won't try to describe the veld further, for it is a totally alien landscape to someone used to the green rolling hills of southern England; a wonderful, visually stunning, environment – one that I have come to love dearly, and which I know Ma loved too. I've walked in a dry dusty donga, and now understand why Ma got homesick in England!

One of the most gratifying experiences of this whole early period of discovery was in watching the interaction between the next generation of the Wellington family: the cousins. Helen and I had already met Fee and Rob's daughter Shirley, and her family in London, but Abi had not been present due to work commitments. She first met her cousin Laura, Fevvy's daughter of the same age, in Port Elizabeth and watching the way in which the two 'lookalikes' took to each other was one of the trip's greatest pleasures. She also met Fee's eldest son, David, another cousin, and again the interaction was as if they had known each other for years. Here were four more new cousins for Abi to meet, including Shirley and her family, and it was to be during our big trip to Cape Town that these meetings would occur.

I could write a book just about the experiences of that one road-trip, but I have not set out to produce a travel guide. Far more I wish to convey the emotions the meetings evoked. Yes, the

Garden Route which spans the 500 miles between Port Elizabeth and the Cape, justifies its position on the tourist 'must see' list of destinations, but I must not dwell on its beauty.

We drove west past the mountains of the Tsitsikamma and Outeniqua ranges, stopping to break the journey for two days at the Knysna natural lagoon, and finally descended the Sir Lowry's Pass, seeing Cape Town and its majestic Table Mountain in the distance.

Two major occasions were to dominate the 'discovery list' here: a big family braai at Cousin Arthur Wellington's, who had originally phoned Fee with the news of my existence; and a big family wedding. Fee's youngest daughter, Heather, was getting married in Paarl in the wine region just outside Cape Town, an event at which there would be no less than seventeen immediate family members. My initiation as a Wellington was about to be raised to another level.

Through the course of our time in the Cape, I was met and welcomed by the entire extended family. From the initial meeting with Arthur and his wife in the beautiful surroundings of the Groot Constantia winery, to the 'gathering of the clan' at the Paarl wedding, all were just so positive and loving. Many of the family had followed the story right from the initial contact in October and were as thrilled in meeting us, as all three of us 'Bradleys' were in meeting them.

Cousin Arthur's braai was an especially emotional occasion. Arthur was the first member of the whole family to whom I had spoken, and he had also provided the final link to my sisters, a task I'm sure, having seen my photographs, he enjoyed! Also Arthur had invited to the braai Steve Hrabar, who had played such a vital role in the closing stages of my searching, having done such a great job listing the Wellington family on the 1820 Settler website AND including his email address. Without him, I wonder if I would ever have found my family. It really was one of the great breakthroughs and for his work and help I will be forever grateful. Some of Arthur's immediate family were present and Cousin Penny had flown down from Johannesburg with many pieces of Wellington memorabilia. On his extremely large dining table, Arthur had laid out the incredible complete family tree. How can I describe the emotion of seeing the recent addition, 'Ralph Allan Wellington'? We discussed much family history, especially that relating to Ma and our grandfather and I told the story of my search many times over. It was during conversations at both this braai and at Heather's wedding, that the idea for this book was born. The requests were not just from friends, but from so many Wellington family members themselves. 'You have to get this all down for the future generations: you must write a book!'

Abi especially was overjoyed at having met all of her six cousins. Her welcome was total, a loving acceptance by the blood relations she had so long wished to have. The photograph, taken at Heather's wedding, of all seven cousins together, is something she will cherish forever. That special bond which so often exists between cousins continued to grow.

I remember, during the beautiful drive back to Port Elizabeth via the old mountain road through Worcester and Swellendam, that almost unreal feeling I had experienced all those months ago when I had first found Ma's name on the shipping list. I had to pinch myself yet again to make sure I was not in that dream world where one's desires simply become reality.

We had several days relaxing in Port Elizabeth before setting off again. We were exhausted both emotionally and from the long journey back from the Cape. Much of the time was spent revising our research into grandfather Arthur Wellington's time as Governor of Healdtown and the family life there and in Hogsback. Fee and Fevvy had been extremely busy before I arrived in South Africa and although they had sent a lot of this information in email format, it was totally different, and far more rewarding, discussing it all with them face to face. There was an awful lot to take on board!

At last we left for the journey back into the Wellington roots at Hogsback and Healdtown – Helen and I, Fee and Rob, Fevvy and Adrian and of course, the lookalike cousins, Abi and Laura. Shirley and her family were to be there as well. No one wished to miss this trip to the mountains.

The road to Hogsback from Port Elizabeth passes through breath-taking scenery, much of it steeped in the history of both the family and the 1820 settlers. An hour and a bit into the journey we stopped in Grahamstown with its array of beautiful, historic buildings. Both my sisters attended Rhodes University as did our grandmother, Muriel Turner, who in 1909 was one of the first women students to be admitted. Grandfather was a young minister in the town and warden at one of the Rhodes hostels until his marriage to Muriel in 1911. (He had known her since his early days ministering in Somerset East – we found proof that by early 1905, when Muriel was only fourteen, they were already fond of each other.) Our research had shown too that her ancestors had settled close to Grahamstown, having sailed from England in 1820, so it was here that I realised I was closing in on my roots.

From Grahamstown the road snakes through the heights of the Ecca Pass, crosses the Great Fish River Valley and finally weaves its way into Fort Beaufort. Here it was that Ma herself had entered the world on 29th July, 1927. I had spent so many years searching for her, knowing only about my own birth, and here I was at the very location of hers. I knew Healdtown was just a couple of miles away up the valley. That unreal feeling crept in again and I gave myself another pinch.

We drove through Alice, where Nelson Mandela had studied at Fort Hare University after leaving Healdtown, and finally turned onto the Hogsback Road.

Hogsback is a wonderful, magical place that sits high in the Amathole Mountains hidden amongst the majestic trees of the indigenous forest. Before 1932, access to it had been extremely difficult, but in that year a pass was built. It was after this that many of the teachers from the mission stations of Lovedale and Healdtown built their holiday homes up at Hogsback in order to escape the dry summer heat. Grandfather Arthur Wellington built his house, Trewennan, at this time, and his sister, Maggie, together with her husband Tom Nicholls, built theirs a few years later. I knew this place was going to be very special.

As we travelled, the Hogsback mountains – the Three Hogs – which have provided such an iconic background to so many family photographs, became my quest. I kept peering ahead, longing to see them. When finally they came into full view I had to ask Adrian to stop the car and let me out so that I could spend that moment alone, drinking in the scene. The image of those three peaks had been so ingrained in my mind that I felt I had actually been there before. This was the view that Ma had loved so much. I cannot really explain my emotions at that moment. I felt I'd come home. It was from these very mountains that the Lady of Shalott had ventured so many years ago to board her ship and to sail away. She had journeyed from this place to Port Elizabeth and then on to England, not knowing she carried me with her.

Trewennan is still there at the end of the lane bearing the same name – only the house itself is different, the original wooden structure which grandfather built having burnt to the ground in 1960 when someone broke in and knocked over a candle. This was a place that had been central to Wellington family life for thirty years. Ma and her brothers had known it since they were children. Fevvy had even been christened in its garden. Everything had been lost, Granny's treasured possessions along with numerous family photographs. (Who can tell what secrets were lost in the flames?) We were welcomed into the garden by the then current owners of the property and it was a very strange feeling. Here were the same trees which I recognised from long ago family pictures, larger now and obscuring the view of the valley below. In the garden, the red-brick bread oven, erected by grandfather, still stood proudly amongst the azaleas, though moss-covered now and unused for decades. After the fire, the property stood empty for many years until Ma finally decided to sell it – this must have been a very difficult decision at the time, one I am sure Ma really didn't wish to make. She knew by then that 'Luke' had retired and had moved back to Hogsback permanently. He had once loved Ma, years before she travelled to England in 1949, and they had even been engaged for a while. She had told Fee and Fevvy that he had continued to love and pursue her even after they had broken up. How could she spend time living in such close proximity to one who had never known of the son he had fathered or the anguish he had caused her? She could never tell him. This most certainly contributed to her decision to sell.

Fee, Ralph and Fevvy. Hogsback, 2012

I remember I stood in the garden at Trewennan thinking of the past there in Hogsback, of Christmas and New Year 1949... what really was the whole truth? With both Ma and 'Luke' having passed away, I resigned myself to the fact that we would never know.

We spent time in Hogsback simply enjoying its beauty, visiting the waterfalls and walking the forest trails Ma herself had loved so much. We were tempted to climb the highest of the three mountains, Hog 1, but decided to leave that achievement for another time – only the young cousins conquered the peak on that occasion. Fee had been here on holiday in 2003 when Ma was very ill and had actually been on the top of Hog 1 when the call came from Fevvy to say that Ma had died. That climb was to be very special – it could wait. (Finally, a few years later, we did all stand together at the top of that peak, saying 'Ma, can you see us?')

We visited Trewedna, once the home of Great Aunt Maggie

and her husband, Tom. The garden, once loved and beautiful was now overgrown and neglected sadly since Tom and Maggie died. Yet it was another garden that was to have such a profound effect on both Helen and myself.

By far the most emotional moment at Hogsback for me came once we had decided to visit 'Luke's' garden. Hogsback is famous for its gardens. The location and altitude led many of the early residents to create gardens reminiscent of their roots in England. The tender plants from the far Northern Hemisphere would grow here in abundance alongside the more usual indigenous South African plants. We knew 'Luke' had created one of the finest gardens and we were given permission from the current owners to visit.

I am very proud of my own garden so far away in the Sussex countryside. Over the years I have used at least six tons of landscape rock to form the basis of a garden planted in a very English style, mainly featuring rhododendrons, azaleas and hydrangeas. There is a large pond in which my beloved carp glide lazily throughout the day, all this linked with rock-lined pathways. Entering 'Luke's' garden had such an effect on me... I actually froze. Helen later said she could 'feel the hair on her neck rising'. Here was *my* garden, but on a vast scale, laid out by a real master and here in the mountains of far-away South Africa. It was breath-taking, the rock pathways carefully created to enhance the views of the wealth of plants, trees and shrubs so perfectly selected for this elevated environment. Here, on a grander scale, were the same plants, the same rocks and the same water features I had so carefully laid out at home. Helen later said that given the same patch of land, it was exactly what I would have strived to create and how correct she was. How could this creation of such beauty have so profoundly influenced my own humble efforts some five thousand miles to the north? The deep mysteries of genetics I will never understand. My sisters have since referred to my garden in England as 'the Mini-Hogsback'.

Our stay at Hogsback was coming to an end but there was one further visit to be made, possibly the most important of all for us three siblings – to Healdtown.

The ruins of the Healdtown mission school stand at the head of the Healdtown kloof, just nine kilometres to the north of Fort Beaufort. (It was down this valley that Ma travelled each day to school in Fort Beaufort, riding on a donkey.) I had only seen one photograph of the mission station, the now famous Mandela picture from 1938. Apart from that, the only other image I had seen was the 1945 painting of the Governor's house and garden which now hung in Fee and Rob's Karoo farmhouse, so I was totally unprepared for the devastation which greeted us as we arrived on the school campus. What had once been, in the words of Nelson Mandela, 'graceful ivy covered Colonial buildings and tree shaded courtyards' had become a sad collection of ruined shells, roofless and open to the elements. It no longer gave the 'feeling of a privileged academic oasis', as Mr Mandela had described. Saddest of all was the Governor's house where our Ma grew up, now nearing collapse and so different from the beautiful house in the painting. It was a sobering experience for the three of us to venture into the very ruins in which the family had lived, avoiding the deep holes between what was left of the floorboards. Here Ma had both worked and played, growing from a little girl to a young woman. As Trevor Webster says in his delightful book, *Healdtown, Under the Eagle's Wings*, Ma 'loved living at Healdtown, to her it was a wonderful place. She was 17 years old when her father died. It was a huge wrench for both her and her mother, Muriel, when they had to move out of the Governor's house and leave it all behind. This had been her home for her whole life.' How devastated Ma would have been to see it as it was now, derelict and unloved.

On the left is the back of the Governor's house and next to it the ruins of the dining hall where the Mandela photo was taken. On the right, standing where Mandela stood.

As we walked slowly through the ruins of the mission station, I reflected on what a legacy grandfather and Healdtown had left to South Africa. I remembered how during the course of my original search for the family I had read so much about this place and its direct influence on how South Africa developed. Now here I was treading in the footsteps of truly great men. The 'academic oasis' had not of course been created by the buildings alone, but far more by the staff who lived and worked there.

Grandfather had been appointed to Healdtown as Governor in 1927. Later, in 1937, whilst he was also President of the Conference of the Methodist Church of South Africa, he appointed Rev. Seth Mokitimi as chaplain and housemaster. Rev Mokitimi was to stay at Healdtown for fifteen years, becoming very much grandfather's right-hand man. In his excellent book, *Mr. President*, covering all the presidents of the Methodist Church, David Sadler states, 'a very special and close relationship grew between Seth and the Reverend A.A. Wellington. Seth said that Wellington loved him and treated him like a brother and he loved "the Duke" or "Gov" as he called Mr. Wellington.' These two had the utmost respect for each other and their discussions were on equal terms. It was observing one of these somewhat heated discussions that was to so influence the young Nelson

Mandela, who later wrote, 'Rev Mokitimi impressed us for another reason: he stood up to Rev Wellington'. He stated that it was witnessing this that made him realise 'a Black man did not have to defer automatically to a White, however senior he was'. How grandfather would love to have witnessed the long-reaching effects this would ultimately have on the man and the country.

Penny Wellington had written to us during our initial research:

> I know for a fact that The Rev, our grandfather, was held
> in high esteem by many Black people who knew him. I
> want to share a story with you. In 1988 when we took our
> son, Lloyd, to Kingswood College, we went to the Wimpy
> in Grahamstown for a hamburger. Sitting at the table next
> to us was a Black family with a small boy also wearing
> K.C. school uniform. Doug held out his hand to greet
> them (as he always did), and said 'I am Doug Wellington.
> I'm pleased to meet you.' The older man in the group
> replied, 'So you are Mr Wellington – Any relation of the
> late Rev. Wellington?' So Doug acknowledged that yes, he
> was a grandson. To this the man's face just lit up. He told
> us that many years before, as a young man, he had worked
> at Healdtown. And he said, 'What a pleasure for me to
> meet the grandson of that good man the Rev. Wellington.
> And to know that today our offspring are going to the
> same school together makes this a very proud day for me!'
> Needless to say, both Doug and I were very touched.
> In the early 60s, when I was training to qualify as a
> radiographer at the Frere Hospital in East London, and
> also later on while I worked in Grahamstown, there were
> often Black patients with the Christian name of
> Wellington. On questioning them, it would invariably be
> because of the Rev Wellington. And what greater

compliment could there be than this. To honour him by naming one's son after him.

He was certainly loved by the local people, who lived (and worked) in the immediate area of the school.

We had one last and important task to complete and that involved a short walk away from the ruins of Healdtown and up to the grave of our grandfather, next to the hillside village there. As we all made our way up the hill, I tried to picture the same scene in 1944 when grandfather had died. According to a printed report from the time of the funeral ceremony, 'the coffin, preceded by the Manyano women and followed by the Ministers, was carried by the students through the playing fields and across the boundary stream and up to the village. Here, at their special request, it was taken by loving village friends who carried it to the enclosed plot which they had given to the Wellington family in perpetuity as a precious token of their gratitude.'

Here we were now, so many years later, walking the same ground, that very same route up to our grandfather's grave.

It is unforgiving ground, stony, dusty ground and hard to cultivate, but here it was that grandfather so wished to be buried overlooking his beloved Healdtown. As we walked up the hill, I remembered what Fevvy had once written to me.

One of my favourite stories about Healdtown happened when our grandfather, Arthur Wellington, had just died. Ma told us how she, just a teenager, had to stand next to his open coffin while an endless stream of mourners filed past, because she was the only one who could do it – it was during the war, and all her brothers were away fighting 'up north'. Granny, meanwhile, became worried that the grave was not being dug. She asked the village Headmen about it. (It was going to be a huge funeral.)

They replied that the ground up on the Healdtown hillside was hard – it was in the middle of a drought – but that they would wait, explaining, 'When a great man dies, God sends the rain.' Ma said that she and Granny just had to accept that. But she told us that in the middle of the night it began to rain, and it rained and it rained...

Where once there had been just one grave, his grave, there were now more on the hillside. A small cemetery had grown up amongst the rocks, overgrown now with the coarse grasses that abound in this arid place. We had picked wild flowers from what had once been the Governor's house garden and as the tears fell we laid them on his grave.

So I end here, the three of us silently weeping, united in our grief. We stood at our grandfather's headstone with our arms around each other, looking over the grave and down at the mission station spread out in the valley below us, where our dear Ma had grown up. From this very place my Lady of Shalott had started out on life's great journey and now, so very many years later, I had returned together with those I had come to love so very much.

Finally, I knew I really did belong.

Acknowledgements

Firstly, thank you to everyone who appears in this story and without whom neither the quest nor the story would exist.

Thanks to Gary and Kath Middleton for allowing me to turn their front room into a likeness of my house in 1961 for the front-cover picture – and to Harley for his excellent impersonation of me at twelve.

Thanks to all those guinea pigs who read the manuscripts as the book progressed and gave me so much help, encouragement and advice.

Thanks to my wife Helen for putting up with me and to my daughter Abi who gave me so much encouragement to continue throughout the later years of my quest. Without her, I would doubtless have resigned myself to failure and given up.

Thanks are also due to Claire Wingfield for her sterling work in actually getting this book published, an area of expertise of which we knew nothing.

Finally, thanks to all the wonderful members of the Wellington family, especially my two sisters, Fee and Fevvy who, between them, of course, have written a substantial part of this book. Since that monumental period during October of 2011, we have shared so much time together both in the UK and South Africa. I have never been so happy and contented.

If you enjoyed this book, please help to spread the word by leaving a review on Amazon, Goodreads, Waterstones online or any other suitable forum. These are a huge help to authors.

You can also visit www.theralphstory.com for updates and exclusive content.

Printed in Great Britain
by Amazon

78448880R00146